beyond the crystal ball

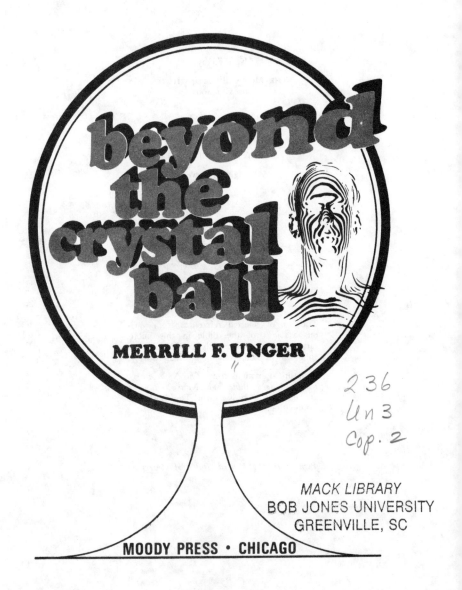

beyond the crystal ball

MERRILL F. UNGER

MOODY PRESS • CHICAGO

Contents

CHAPTER	PAGE
1. The Crystal Ball Craze	7
2. Latter-Day Demon Activity	17
3. Mystical Babylon Materializes	29
4. Millions Vanish in a Moment	42
5. The Saints Rewarded in Glory	55
6. Rome Revives	69
7. The Russian Bear Rampages	81
8. China's Millions March	96
9. Tribulation Engulfs the Earth	105
10. The War That Ends War	118
11. Christ Returns to Judge Sinners	128
12. God's Great Society Established	139
13. Hell and the Fate of the Wicked	152
14. Heaven and the Destiny of the Redeemed	166
15. Don't Fall into the Occult Trap	179
Notes	186

1

The Crystal Ball Craze

THE DECADE OF THE SEVENTIES has been called the dawn of the occult era, the "age of Aquarius."[1] A revival of interest in psychic phenomena is everywhere evident. People want to know the future. A sorrowing widow attends a seance, seeking to communicate with the spirit of her deceased husband. A distinguished churchman, rejecting Christian supernaturalism, turns to spiritualism to consult the spirit of his departed son, a victim of drug addiction.[2] A distraught wife, abandoned by her husband, seeks solace in the horoscope and the study of astrology.

A VACUUM TO BE FILLED

Widespread apostasy in the present-day church has left a colossal spiritual emptiness in the hearts of millions. As air rushes in to fill a vacuum, powerful forces are vying to occupy the void left in men's lives by the abandonment of the Christian faith. As the result of the failure of the contemporary church to envision its true spiritual dimension and power, multitudes are seeking direction and help from organizations that foster psychic phenomena and experiences.

Popular today are such movements as Spiritual Frontiers Fellowship (SFF), Inner Peace Movement (IPM), The Association for Research and Enlightenment (ARE), and The Religious Research Foundation of America (RRFA). Pathetically, the empty soul of modern man, devoid of faith in God, is trying to satisfy itself with the husks of materialism and godless pleasure. Utterly disillusioned,

7

it is succumbing to the lure of spiritualism and is being captivated by the delusive call of the occult.

Ancient Prophets — True and False

Whether a prophet is true or false is a guessing game, unless one follows Scripture. There specific criteria are given to make an objective evaluation.

In ancient Israel, pretending to be a prophet of God was a serious matter. The death penalty was dealt to the would-be prognosticator who dared to speak in the Lord's name something the Lord had not commanded him, or who presumed to predict future events "in the name of other gods" (Deu 18:20). In the former case, he would be branded as a false prophet parading as a true prophet of the Lord. In the latter instance, he would be exposed as an unashamed false prophet, blatantly imposing his deception upon the Lord's people.

On the other hand, the true prophet of the Lord *always* spoke truth. He uttered predictions that never foundered, even in the slightest detail. The criterion of genuineness was not the prophet's claim to speak from the Lord, but the *complete* fulfillment of his predictions (Deu 18:21-22). God never makes blunders or misses the mark. His arrows of truth always hit the bull's-eye.

Modern Prophets and Prognosticators

In our era, the ancient prophets of the Bible are bypassed. Modern predicters of the future are avidly followed. Jeanne Dixon is listened to by millions to whom Isaiah, Jeremiah, and Daniel are unfamiliar names. Edgar Cayce, "the sleeping prophet," and Maurice Woodruff, called "astrology's brightest star,"[3] are eagerly read and consulted by millions who know little or nothing concerning the prophecies of Jesus, or of John, the author of the Revelation.

Sybil Leek, self-styled "the most famous witch in the world," is only one of the brighter luminaries in an ever increasing galaxy of lesser lights who undertake to peer behind the curtain that veils the future. Manhattan alone boasts more than five hundred witches.[4] Today fortune-telling is big business.

Psychic literature is flooding the market. The theater, movies, radio, and television are honeycombed with occult themes and allusions. Astrology and spiritualism lead the van. Popular also are tarot card reading, tumbler moving, ouija board manipulation, automatic writing, materializations, spiritistic visions, palm reading, and excursions of the psyche.

Yet Scripture takes account of the fact that false prophets and psychic clairvoyants *also* predict things that come to pass. They may actually attain a high degree of predictive marksmanship. A sign or wonder of prognostication, therefore, is not in itself a proof that God has spoken. God allows false prophets a *restricted* degree of power through demonic agency to foretell the future. The purpose of this is to *test* the love and loyalty of His people for Him (Deu 13:1-3).

But what are the tests that distinguished the true prophet of the Lord from the psychic clairvoyant? The first test is *accuracy*. God's prophets were one hundred percent accurate. They, in contrast to the frequent misses of the pagan seer, always hit the mark dead center (Deu 18:20-22).

The second test is *obedience*. Strict adherence to the Word of God and the will of God was the only sure safeguard against imposition and consequent delusion from false prophets. If they taught in the name of pagan deities, they were openly and obviously in rebellion against God and easily recognized. If they taught in God's name, but disregarded God's Word and will, they were secretly and more insidiously in rebellion (Deu 13:4-9). In either case, because of the danger to God's people, death was the penalty (Deu 13:5).

Modern Prophets — The True and the False

Unfortunately, the problem of the false prophet versus the true voice of the Lord is not confined to antiquity. It has plagued every era of the history of the fallen race. It presses upon us today with peculiar urgency.

Our Lord Himself solemnly warned that at the end of the age, false Christs and false prophets would arise and perform such miracles and feats of prognostication that even His own elect people would succumb to overpowering deception, except for His over-ruling grace and power (Mt 24:24).

The Spirit, through the apostle Paul, pointedly declares that such false prophets would depart from the faith. Under demon power, their consciences seared, they would promulgate doctrines instigated by demons (1 Ti 4:1-3).

The apostle John pleads with the Lord's beloved not to listen to the demon spirits energizing these false teachers (1 Jn 4:1). The apostle James characterizes the uncanny knowledge these clair-voyants possess as not heavenly in origin — that is, inspired by the Holy Spirit — but earthly, natural, and dictated by demonic spirits (Ja 3:15). The apostle Peter exposes the craft and deceit of these false teachers (2 Pe 2:1-22). Jude also sternly denounces them (Jude 3-19).

THE TEST OF THE TRUE PROPHET TODAY

A motley babel of prophets on the contemporary scene vie with one another to be heard. In the clamor of alien voices, the question, What voice is that of a true spokesman for God? is of the utmost importance. As would be expected, the Scriptures are transparently explicit on a point so vital to the welfare of a believer. The New Testament gives clear-cut criteria enabling the child of God to differentiate between truth and error.

The true spokesman for God speaks according to the Word of God. Now that the Scriptures have been completed in written form since about A.D. 100, and available to God's people for study, the first-century gifts of direct extrabiblical prophecy and knowledge have been superseded by God's completed record of revelation (1 Co 13:8). This is the "completed [final] thing" (Greek), referred to by Paul in his discussion of the permanent versus the nonperma-nent gifts (1 Co 13:9-10).

Now the claim to prophetic visions received outside of and apart from the written Word of God is to be regarded as highly suspect. Predictions by Jeanne Dixon, Sibyl Leek, Maurice Wood-ruff, or any of the numerous seers, astrologers, mediums, and clair-voyants that are currently flourishing, fall into this category.

All that God has made known regarding the future is now recorded in His "sure word of prophecy" (2 Pe 1:19). Now a New Testament "prophet" is no more than an expositor of these recorded prophecies. The early apostolic gift of direct inspirational prophecy and knowledge was piecemeal and partial for such occasion of need. For this very reason, the apostle declared these gifts would be superseded. And they have been, by the completed, final, recorded revelation.

However, it must be remembered, God is sovereign and omnipotent. He does not place Himself in a straitjacket. In the matter of spiritual gifts, He operates on a twofold basis. Does the exercise of the gift glorify Him? Is there a human need for the manifestation of it? If there is a human need and the gift is exercised to meet that need, God will be glorified. Moreover, the directives of His Word do not nullify this fact.

In uncivilized lands where the converted nationals are illiterate or have no Scripture in their own language, God is perfectly free to endow certain of His own with the apostolic gifts of prophecy and knowledge. However, this situation would be rare. It would happen only if the missionary, who introduced the people to Christ, for some reason could not remain and teach them from the Scriptures he possessed in his own language. In such an instance, there would be a parallel to the apostolic assemblies of the first century before the New Testament Scriptures came into being and began to circulate among the churches.

There is a difference, however, between the two situations. In the case of the apostolic assemblies, the truths revealed and given by the Spirit were those which were eventually to be written down to become available to the churches. In the case of the present-day missionary need, the truths revealed to the illiterate people would be those already recorded in the once-for-all revelation contained in the Bible, but not available to them through the written medium.

God's Yardstick to Measure Truth

In the ecumenical atmosphere of the times, it is customary to view one religion to be as good as another. The idea of a God-revealed body of truth, fully inspired and authoritative, as the Holy Scriptures have always been regarded by Christians, is distasteful to today's world. There is a determination to cast off all restraint imposed by anything claimed to be "the only infallible rule of faith and practice." In the age of Aquarius, a fully inspired and authoritative Bible is being rejected. As a result, perversions of Christianity flourish. The Christian mission is held to be a seeking of truth in dialogue with the adherents of non-Christian faiths, rather than a proclamation of truth which God has supernaturally revealed in the Bible.

A practical question naturally arises. Does God have the answer to the interminable religious confusion of our times? The answer is emphatically yes! He has furnished the believer a yardstick to measure his way through the exceedingly complex realm of the religious.

This yardstick is found in 1 Timothy 3:15. It includes (1) the incarnation — God became a man — "God was manifested in the flesh"; (2) Christ's death and resurrection — "He was justified in the Spirit"; (3) Christ's divine person and redemptive work attested by the elect unfallen angelic creation — "seen by angels"; (4) the efficacy of Christ's redemptive work demonstrated — He was "believed on in the world"; (5) the divine seal set upon Christ's redemptive work — He was "received up into glory."

Any teaching that denies or comes into conflict with the criteria of truth found in this digest of essential Christian verities must be branded as error instigated by demon powers and categorized as "doctrines of devils" (1 Ti 4:1).

TEST OF GOD'S SPIRIT

Demon spirits energizing false prophets are adept at parading as the Spirit of God energizing the true prophets of God. Only the strict application of the test recorded by John can differentiate between the two (1 Jn 4:1-2). Every spirit that genuinely and sincerely owns and submits to the fact that Jesus Christ is God incarnate is from God. This confession means that he owns that Jesus Christ was virgin born, sinless in life, vicarious in death, victorious in resurrection, and that He carried His glorified humanity to heaven as the world's Saviour and mankind's Redeemer.

Every spirit who refuses to own and submit to this great central truth of the divine-human nature of Christ's Person and His consequent Saviourhood is a demon spirit in open rebellion against God. This is the spirit of Antichrist that is the hallmark of all false doctrine and religion (1 Jn 4:3).

This test draws the dividing line between spiritual truth and error. It supplies the criterion to separate the false teacher from the true. It sets forth Christianity not as *a* religion, but as *the* religion, not as *a* way to God but the *only* way to God. It nips the error of the ecumenical movement in the bud. It furnishes the sound foundation for the structure of spiritual truth. It is the starting point for evaluating the cults of Christianity and in judging *all* the non-Christian religions of the world.

WITCH-STONING AND WITCH-BURNING

Witch-stoning under the Mosaic law was evidently a necessity to warn ancient Israel of the peril of contamination from the depraved occult-ridden religion of the Canaanites. To survive as a God-called nation, Israel had to destroy or be destroyed. God's people had to separate themselves from evil or be engulfed by it (Deu 18:9-14).

Periodic outbursts of witch-baiting in medieval and modern times, particularly the witch-burning in colonial America at Salem, Massachusetts, in the latter part of the eighteenth century, are to be considered as misdirected and the result of fanaticism. While witchcraft has lost none of its evil and God-dishonoring aspects in the passing of the centuries, the Mosaic death penalty applied to ancient Israel only. Even there it was imposed to offset a particular peril presented by the debauched, demonized religion of the Canaanites.

REVIVAL OF WITCHCRAFT TODAY

Occultism has been cultivated from dim antiquity. In certain areas in particular, such as Switzerland and parts of Germany and France, witches and clairvoyants for many centuries have sharpened their gaze into human destiny and attempted to foretell the future by the study of the magical arts. Occult literature which instructs in magic and fortune-telling, such as the celebrated, so-called Sixth and Seventh Books of Moses, has circulated in Europe since before the Reformation.

Because of the dominance of Christianity, such practices were abhorred and engaged in only in the dark. Now, however, in the present-day occult explosion, the magical arts are being proudly paraded in theater, movies, television, radio, and in the literature of the day. Traditional "Christian" society, as a result of large-scale departure from biblical Christianity, is opening the floodgates to an inundation of witchcraft, magic, sorcery, tarot card reading, seances, spiritism, and astrology, that is unparalleled. Never has the crystal ball been so highly polished and popular or the Bible been so neglected.

Witches in Manhattan

In the January 9, 1970 issue of *Life* appeared a picture of Elizabeth, described as being one of 500 witches residing in Manhattan alone. Elizabeth claims to be a white — or "good" — witch, as opposed to black, or evil, witches. This alleged distinction evidences the fact that she heeds the crystal ball and not the Bible. The latter brands all witchcraft as evil. White magic, with its religious veneer, is just as demonic as black magic, which shamelessly subscribes to Satan and evil spirits. The source and dynamic of both are identical.[5]

Elizabeth learned the witch's craft from her mother, who was also a witch. She reads tarot cards, attends coven meetings, casts spells, and makes constant use of incantations. Her goal, like all witches, is to gain supernatural knowledge and enlist supernatural power.

The evil of witchcraft is obvious to the Bible reader. The knowledge and power the witch seeks is independent of God and in opposition to the Word of God. Moreover, it is sought by methods that are unsanctioned by God and dishonoring to Him.

WHAT'S WRONG WITH FORTUNE TELLING?

Man has always possessed a natural curiosity about the future, but the past few years have witnessed an unbelievable upsurge of public interest in what lies beyond today. In addition to all previously mentioned occultic practices, newsstands are flooded with literature on the subject. Preparing and publishing horoscopes is big business.

How is such activity to be evaluated? Is it a mere innocent pastime — a passing fad devoid of moral or spiritual repercussions? Or is it a danger signal, indicating a sick society and foreboding disaster ahead?

The answer to this question depends upon whether one puts his confidence in the Holy Bible or the horoscope, whether one is trusting in the inspired Scriptures or the crystal ball of the spiritistic clairvoyant.

The Word of God is decisive. It categorizes all mediumistic fortune-tellers and clairvoyant prognosticators as the offshoot of ancient pagan idolatry or modern godless secularism. Spiritistic mediums and clairvoyants are revealed to be traffickers in demon-energized paganism (Lev 17:7; Deu 32:17; Ps 106:37; 1 Co 10:20; Rev 9:20-21).

To attend a seance or to consult a medium or clairvoyant concerning the future is a defiling thing for God's people, insulting to the Lord their God (Lev 19:31). Such an act sets aside God's Word and the full prophetic revelation set forth there.

In seeking knowledge of the future, independent of God's Word or in opposition to it, or using means to obtain such knowledge forbidden or unsanctioned by God, is to affront His deity. It breaks the first commandment of God's eternal moral law, reflected in the Mosaic Decalogue, enjoining supreme love and loyalty to the Lord (Ex 20:1-6).

For this reason, occultism in any form is a serious sin. Under the Mosaic law, it incurred God's stern punishment and resulted in the implicated one being cut off from the Lord's people (Ex 20:6;

Lev 20:6). Spiritistic mediumship incurred the death penalty by stoning (Lev 20:27).

GOD'S TELESCOPE TO PIERCE THE FUTURE

In a day when clairvoyants and witches are becoming as common as Santa Clauses at Christmas, God alone has the true answer to the future. His Word is an X ray. It not only analyzes us within the soul, it shows us what we are and will be. His prophetic Word is a telescope. It foretells for us what lies ahead, both in time and in eternity. Within the pages of the Holy Scriptures is recorded all we need to know and should know regarding the future.

Because men are rejecting God's Word, they are turning to mediums and clairvoyants. Disobeying God's voice, like King Saul (1 Sa 28:3, 7), they are turning to false prophets and alien voices inspired by demonic spirits (1 Ti 4:1-2; 1 Jn 4:1-2). Forfeiting the analysis of themselves and the knowledge of what's ahead that God's Word furnishes, they are resorting to knowledge of the future forbidden by the Holy Scriptures.

Man's desire to know the future cries out to be satisfied. In days of crisis and impending world upheaval, men must know, and are determined to know, what lies ahead. If God will not answer them, the devil will (1 Sa 28:6, 8). Never has humanity faced a more urgent challenge. The Holy Bible or the crystal ball are humanity's alternatives in the age of Aquarius.

2

Latter-Day Demon Activity

ONE OF THE MOST AMAZING ASPECTS of biblical prophecy is the prediction of a vast increase in the activity of demons in the last days of this age. This disclosure has, of course, been found in the New Testament from the time of its inception. The truth it contains, however, has not been adequately recognized or expounded until comparatively recent times.

In 1950, Wilbur M. Smith first called clear attention to the predicted rise of demon power in the end time.[1] In 1952, I published a doctrinal exposition of the teaching of the Scriptures on the subject of demons, entitled *Biblical Demonology*.[2] In 1971, I published a study of the experiential aspects of the subject called *Demons in the World Today*.[3] At present, the church is being alerted to the peril of demonic forces as they are manifest in apostasy, occultism, lawlessness, immorality, violence, and world unrest.

REAL DEMONS TODAY?

Unfortunately, the alert concerning the danger of demonic spirits in the end time is being heeded by comparatively few. Sophisticated unbelief in Christian circles scarcely entertains the idea of a personal devil, much less that of personal beings called demons. In non-Christian circles, the whole subject is viewed as pure superstition, except where occultism is cultivated as a form of religion. There, evil supernaturalism is comprehended as a fearful reality.

Satan and demons become as real to the occultist and spiritist

17

as God and the elect unfallen angels are to the Christian. This is true whether the spirits parade as angels of light under the guise of white magic or as the wicked spirits they really are and enlisted as such under the undisguised evil of black magic.[4]

Real demons exist today because magic is practiced today, as it has been from antiquity. And magic is nothing more than diabolic miracle — the use of supernatural power apart from God and in opposition to God.

Magic and the End of the Age

The prophetic Word reveals that the Holy Spirit indwelling the church corporately and the believer individually prevents the full manifestation of demonic magic (2 Th 2:1-7). It also discloses that when the church is completed and presented by the Spirit to Christ in heaven as a glorified entity, the Spirit's ministry of restraining lawlessness upon the earth will be to a large degree removed.

The Spirit's departure with the completed church will be in the same sense as His advent to form it at Pentecost (Jn 14:16; 16:13; Ac 2:1-4). This event will occasion an unprecedented outburst of demonic magic as the age rushes to its close (2 Th 2:8-12).

Latter-day magic will focus in the personal Antichrist, the man of lawlessness (Rev 13:1-11). Satan and demonic powers will operate through him with magical power and every conceivable supernatural sign and deceiving wonder (2 Th 2:8-9).

The purpose of this terrible eruption of demonism will be judicial. God will allow it to bring judgment upon those who, during the last days of the church, displayed no love for the truth. They rejected God's Word and its gospel of salvation. Now they will be turned over to overpowering occult deception to believe Satan's lie, the Antichrist (2 Th 2:10-12).

Enter Jannes and Jambres

These are two of the magicians who opposed Moses and the Word of God in the contest with Pharaoh of Egypt (2 Ti 3:8). They prefigure the occult religionists foretold to arise in the "perilous times" of the "last days" (2 Ti 3:1). As they withstood Moses, so those who abandon the Christian faith for occult religionism in the end time will reject and oppose the truth of God.

The astonishing thing, however, is that the resultant falsehoods these practictioners of demonized religion propagate will be supported by a restricted but real show of diabolic miracle.

As God allowed the occultists of Egypt a circumscribed sphere of supernatural feat by demon power (Ex 7:11-12, 22; 8:7; 9:11), these men of depraved mind, reprobate (rejected) concerning the Christian faith (2 Ti 3:8), will deceive their dupes by a similar display of occult phenomena.

An Incredible Prophecy

Jesus uttered it almost two millenniums ago. Today in the dawn of the occult age, when the modern counterparts of Jannes and Jambres are coming to the fore, the stage is being set for its large scale fulfillment.

"Not every one that saith unto me, Lord, Lord, shall enter into the kingdom of heaven, but he that doeth the will of my Father, who is in heaven. Many will say to me in that day, Lord, Lord, have we not prophesied in thy name? And in thy name have cast out demons, And in thy name done many wonderful works? And then will I profess unto them, I never knew you: depart from me, ye that work iniquity" (Mt 7:21-23, NSRB).

What our Lord foresaw are religious leaders who practice white magic. They use the name of God and of Christ and religious terminology. But this is only a camouflage to conceal the demonic nature of their supernatural feats. The lawlessness they engage in is in the spiritual realm. The knowledge they seek and the power they employ are independent of God and in opposition to His Word. The results they achieve are therefore demonic, just as demonic as if, like Jannes and Jambres, they openly subscribed to the evil powers behind pagan gods to practice black magic.

Open Door — Enter Demons

The predicted latter-day upsurge of demon activity is to be made possible by the large-scale abandonment of the inspiration and authority of Holy Scripture. No single theological issue of the twentieth century has been so pivotal as that which has raged about the subject of what place the Bible is to hold in the belief and life of the modern-day Christian.

The fundamentalist-liberal debates of the 1920s and early thirties led to wide rejection of biblical inerrancy and full authority of Scripture. This situation opened the floodgates to the apostasy of the forties and fifties, which in turn produced the God-is-dead theology with its new morality of the sixties. These ominous events were the natural precursors, paving the way for the occult age of the seventies.

The era of the demon and the false prophet is now upon us. Deception, lawlessness, violence, and immorality have become the order of the day and are due to increase (2 Ti 3:1-13).

Underlying the world's present plight is the power of the demon. When man turned his back upon the Word of God (cf. 2 Ti 3:14-17), he opened the door to vicious spirit forces.

The Word of God is the only sure bulwark against demonic incursion. No wonder modern man, considering himself wiser than God, is where he is today.

No wonder demon morals prevail. No wonder demon deception is rampant. No wonder Jannes and Jambres in modern dress are resisting the truth. No wonder present-day religionists are "ever learning, and never able to come to the knowledge of the truth" (2 Ti 3:7). No wonder "evil men and seducers [are becoming] worse and worse, deceiving and being deceived" (2 Ti 3:13).

APOSTASY AND DOCTRINES OF DEMONS

One of the clearest and most solemn predictions of the Spirit of God is the colossal apostasy from the Christian faith that is to characterize the church of the latter times. This departure from revealed truth is declared to be the work of deceiving spirits or demons (1 Ti 4:1). These wicked agencies are foreseen as having a major role in opposing and perverting the Word of God and turning men away from the true Christian faith based upon that Word.

Turning away from the faith, men take up with deluding spirits that operate in demonized religionism. The result is subscription to "doctrines of demons." These are teachings originated by demons and espoused by apostates and heretics. The apostle Paul illustrates such demonic teachings in a type of ascetic legalism, then current (1 Ti 4:2-5).

Apostates are unregenerate religionists, like the late Bishop James A. Pike, who once gave lip service to sound doctrine.[5] Under demonic influence, however, they renounce their alleged faith and yield to doctrines of demons and become exponents of demon-energized religion.

Heretics are truly regenerated believers. As a result of ignorance, false instruction, or unsound interpretation, they come under demon influence and espouse heresy. This reduces their Christian usefulness to the degree demonic forces have been permitted to influence them.

LISTENING TO SPIRITS

Listening to spirits is common in a day of vocal clairvoyants and dynamic false prophets. They who turn away from the faith "give heed to seducing spirits" (1 Ti 4:1). The apostle John foresaw the rapid increase of such "spirit-listeners" at the end of the age (1 Jn 4:3). He therefore warns God's beloved people not to "believe every spirit." Rather they are to "test" the spirits to see whether they issue from God or are demon spirits energizing false prophets (1 Jn 4:1).

Listening to the prophet, declares John, is tantamount to listening to the spirit who energizes the prophet. The prophet or teacher, accordingly, is merely the human agent through whom the spirit speaks.

The Holy Spirit energizes all true spokesmen for God. He needs no assistance from the elect, unfallen angels, since He is both omniscient and omnipotent (1 Jn 4:2; cf. Jn 16:12-13). Spirits not of God (demons) energize false teachers. Since these demons often are similar to and ape good spirits, they must be rigidly tested by criteria centering in the Person and completed redemptive work of Christ (1 Ti 3:16; 1 Jn 4:2).

Testing, or differentiating, the spirits must therefore always accompany listening to spirits. In broadest scope, the revealed Word of God is the fullest test. "To the law and to the testimony: if they speak not according to this word, it is because there is no light in them" (Is 8:20).

SPIRITED RELIGIOUS FADDISTS AND CULTISTS

The Holy Spirit inspires the man of God with zeal and fervor. Demon spirits likewise imbue false prophets with enthusiasm. Doctrines which demons instigate, they are zealous to propagate. The false teacher, religious faddist, and doctrinal blunderbuss, who contribute to the labyrinthian confusion of the modern religious scene, are not people who need to be stirred up.

False teachers commonly possess the zeal of the fanatic. The reason? They are energized by demon spirits (1 Jn 4:1). The demon in turn directs his attack against the Word of God. He tries to deny it, discredit it, pervert it, distort it, or do anything to bring it into disrepute. This is why any half-truth, downright falsehood, lopsided teaching, or seemingly innocent doctrinal hobby enjoys special demonic inspiration.

DEMONS FROM THE BOTTOMLESS PIT

Wicked demons are loose in the world today. These unclean spirits have access to men to influence and indwell those who yield to them. The demoniacs encountered by Jesus during His earthly ministry have their counterparts today, especially in pagan lands and among aboriginal peoples.[6]

However, the most wicked and vicious evil spirits are not now loose. They are imprisoned in the abyss, the prison of the demons (Lk 8:30-31). The apostle John reveals that these depraved denizens of the shadowy world of the occult will be let loose upon wicked earth dwellers at the end of the age after the church has been glorified and removed to heaven (Rev 9:1-12).

These vile spirits, released to energize and torment mankind during the coming time of worldwide trouble, are envisioned as locusts. The symbolism is descriptive of the invisible spirit world in terms visible and comprehensible to men.

When the abyss is opened, a thick smoke issues from it as from a furnace. The apostle sees the demons, like locusts, coming out of the smoke and descending upon the earth to torment men with excruciating pain. The pain they inflict is compared to the sting of a scorpion when it strikes a person.

Only God's people, protected by His divine seal, escape the horrible agony the demons inflict. So crazed with pain will men become that they will seek to commit suicide, but as if to mock their agony, death will flee from them (Rev 9:4-6).

HEYDAY OF THE OCCULT AGE

The occult era of the seventies, now heralded as the age of Aquarius, from the eleventh sign of the Zodiac, will then have come to its frightful fruition.[7] The torment this gigantic demon eruption will inflict upon the human race at the end of the age is physical as well as mental and emotional. But this is only part of the awful agony of Satan-dominated mankind.

Vicious, depraved spirits will indwell men's bodies, which they will use to satisfy their own vile lusts. Men, reduced to abysmal slaves of Satan, will be goaded on to the vilest of sins and reduced to the most shameless degradation.

It is a sobering thought to realize that spirits so vile that they are now imprisoned will one day be let loose to craze and drive rebellious mankind on to its awful age-end career of lawlessness and revolt against God.

Scripture solemnly names the king of these vicious demons from the abyss. From the Hebrew *Abaddon,* the name means destruction (Rev 9:11; cf. Job 26:6; Pr 15:11). The Greek form is *Apollyon,* meaning destroyer (cf. 2 Th 2:7-12).

WHEN DEATH RIDES VICTORIOUS

The loosing of myriads of unclean spirits from the abyss (Rev 9:1-12) signalizes the demonization of a huge army marching from China and the Far East (Rev 9:16-19). This demonized host of 200,000,000 men advances without hindrance from the Orient (from "the sunrising") across the Euphrates River (Rev 16:12). Like the armies that march to Armageddon, this gigantic force is energized by demonic agencies to invade the Holy Land (cf. Dan 11:44).

As a result of the invasion of this huge host, one-third of the earth's population will be wiped out. This will mean over two billion human beings, if the global population at that time is conservatively set at six billion.

Satan, the liar and murderer (Jn 8:44), at that horrible moment will seem to be triumphant, as he works through his myriads of demon helpers.

THE CULT OF THE DEMON WORSHIPERS

The heyday of the occult age, brought to its flood tide by the loosing of the myriads of vile spirits from the abyss, will witness an outburst of Satanism and demon worship unparalleled in world history.

The apocalyptic seer recounts the dreadful scene. "And the rest of the men which were not killed by these plagues yet repented not of the works of their hands, that they should not worship devils, and idols . . . Neither repented they of their murders, nor of their sorceries, nor of their fornication, nor of their thefts" (Rev 9:20-21).

Open submission to Satan with worship of evil spirits prepares men for the grossest idolatry, the dynamic of which is demonism (1 Co 10:20). The demon is first and foremost opposed to God and seeks to turn mankind away from the love and loyalty due only to the Creator (Ex 20:1-6).

Demon worship confirms men in wickedness and rebellion. Those snared in the cult of demon worship are caught in the throes of violence and crime. They do not repent of their murders. Their creed becomes the occult. They do not repent of their sorceries. Sexual immorality becomes their way of life. They do not repent of their fornication. They support themselves by robbery. They do not repent of their thefts.

THE CHURCH OF SATAN

Already in the dawn of the occult age, the cult of the demon worshipers is appearing in its incipient forms. In 1966 a man named Anton La Vey proclaimed the "new satanic age" and the founding of the "church of Satan" in his home in San Francisco, California.

The adherents of this cult subscribe to black magic and curses, and espouse indulgence rather than abstinence. The occult is the creed. Witchcraft, astrology, the tarot, palmistry, and other practices of the psychic realm of evil supernaturalism are the common beliefs and practices of the church of Satan. As high priest, LaVey celebrates satanic masses.[8]

Satanism is, however, a far wider cult than the so-called church of Satan. Its devotees cultivate various pagan rituals. Often the worship is a mixture of ancient fertility rites and ancient occult practices revived in more modern forms.[9]

Unclean Spirits, Like Frogs

Demons, symbolized by noisy croaking creatures from the quagmires of the world, are envisioned by the apocalyptic seer as energizing the armies of the nations in the last great battle of the age. These "spirits of demons" form the delusive means of persuading the nations to assemble for the supreme folly of Armageddon (Rev 16:13-16).

As demon spirits induced Ahab to embark on the foolhardy venture that cost him his life at Ramoth-gilead (1 Ki 22:20-28), these agencies of Satan will engineer the supreme folly of Armageddon. Man will then think to fight against God, annihilate the Jew, banish Christ's name and sovereignty from the earth, and take over the dominion of this planet for himself under Satan.

Man's noisy, empty pretentions to accomplish this vain design under demon inspiration and dynamic are aptly compared to the loud croaking of frogs from the pernicious swamps of the world where they breed.

Enter the Personal Antichrist

The Antichrist is also known as the beast, the Roman prince, the last great ruler of Gentile world power, headed up in revived Rome (Rev 13:1-10). Satan, the dragon, is the dynamic behind the beast. This is the explanation of the beast's complete defiance of God, as he blasphemes God and those who belong to God (Rev 13:6).

The beast makes war against the saints (Dan 7:21-22; Rev 11:7, 12). As devil-indwelt and demon-impelled, he is permitted unrestrained power over all earth dwellers, except the elect. He is Satan's masterpiece of human wickedness.

False Prophet Par Excellence

The man called the false prophet is the Antichrist's prophet, camouflaged as a lamb (Rev 13:11-18). As such he directs the blasphemous worship of the Antichrist with full demonstration of miraculous (magical) powers. He succeeds in giving life to the image of the beast and in killing those who refuse to worship his image.

This sinister personality sums up in himself the acme of occult powers. In him the present occult age will come to fruition. The mystical number 666, the mark of the beast, which he causes men to receive to buy or sell, symbolizes the climax of man's wicked revolt against God and his completed domination by occult powers.

Demons and the Harlot Church

Glorified and removed to heaven, the true church will be followed by the false church on earth. This will be a harlot system, personified by a wicked, licentious, and debauched woman (Rev 17:1-6). She portrays the consummation of the work of evil spirits in turning men away from the Word of God and corrupting and deluding them into "doctrines of demons" (1 Ti 4:1) to follow "false prophets" (1 Jn 4:1).

The woman who heads up the corrupt system of the end time in fullest scope represents all apostate religious movements. In her is seen the operation of Satan and demons in the religious realm from the inception of religious error in ancient Babylon to its terrible consummation in the demonized religionism united in one great ecumenical merger of the end time (Rev 17:7-18).

THE HABITATION OF DEMONS

As ecclesiastical Babylon degenerates into a harlot church of the end time, commercial Babylon is predicted to fall utterly when it in turn becomes "the habitation of demons" (Rev 18:2). Babylon, whether in its religious aspects (Rev 17) or into its godless commercial and economic aspects (Rev 18), is the world system that governs the life of unregenerate mankind organized under Satan and demonic powers.

This evil system is mentioned more than thirty times in the New Testament. Satan is its directing head (Jn 12:31). The system from God's viewpoint is wholly evil (Gal 1:4; Col 1:13; Ja 4:4). It is limited and temporary (1 Jn 4:4), being characterized by greed, pride, and war (Ja 4:1-4).

The satanic world system is doomed to destruction at Christ's second advent (Rev 19:11-16; 20:1-3). Only as it crashes in ruin can God's righteous kingdom be set up upon the earth in the coming age of peace.

CONQUEROR OF THE DEMONS

Christ is then seen coming in power and glory, symbolized by His sitting upon a white horse (Rev 19:11-14). He comes with His glorified, victorious saints to judge and make war against His enemies, who have purposed to take over the globe and banish the name of Christ from the earth (Ps 2:1-12). Coming in vengeance upon His foes, His garments are seen dipped in His enemies' blood (Is 63:1-4).

The Conqueror conquers supernaturally through His omnipotent Word (Is 11:4; Rev 19:15-16). He rules with stern inflexibility and absolute sovereignty. He reigns as absolute King and Lord. He conquers the Satan-dominated demon-crazed earth dwellers and consigns Satan and the demons, who control them, to the bottomless pit.

THE PRISON DOOR CLOSES ON THE DEMONS

The demons are bound with Satan in the abyss, the prison of the demons (Ze 13:2; Lk 8:30-31; Rev 20:1-3). This binding is necessary because Christ's coming kingdom has for its object the restoration of the divine authority over the earth (Ac 15:14-17). The world system ruled over by Satan and demons must therefore be destroyed before Christ's righteous rule is set up.

Satan and demons are loosed for a little season after the millennium (Rev 20:7-9). Then they are cast into eternal hell, never more to trouble a sinless universe (Rev 20:11-15; 21:3).

3

Mystical Babylon Materializes

UNDER THE FIGURATIVE USE of the name of the ancient city of Babylon, the Bible presents one of its most amazing predictions. This forecast concerns the spiritual and religious history of mankind outside the true church of Jesus Christ.

Very clearly, Scripture predicts the direction and destiny of the true church of God during this age. Just as clearly, it foretells the formation and fate of the false church that will be left on the earth after the true church has been glorified and removed to heaven. One is presented as a chaste virgin espoused to Christ (2 Co 11:2; Eph 5:25-27) and to be joined to Him as wife, the figure of marriage portraying glorification with Him.

The other is set forth as an impure woman, a great harlot, figuratively introduced as mystical Babylon. She will be left upon the earth after the true virgin church has been taken away to be joined to Christ in glory (Rev 17).

ANCIENT BABYLON OF NIMROD

The prehistoric city was situated in lower Babylonia. It dominated the alluvial plain of the Tigris-Euphrates basin, which formed the cradle of ancient civilization. In connection with Babylon, earthly imperial power is first introduced in human history and presented with evil connotation (Gen 10:8-10).

Nimrod, the founder of the kingdom of Babylon, was a rebel against God, as his name suggests.* He is also described as "a

---

* The name *Nimrod* is from the Hebrew root *marad*, to be stubbornly resistant to authority (Jos 22:16; Eze 2:3; Dan 9:9). The name "no doubt suggested to the Israelites the idea of 'rebel' . . . against God" (A. Dillmann, *Genesis*, vol. 1, trans. W. B. Stevenson [Edinburgh, 1897], p. 350).

mighty hunter before the LORD" (Gen 10:9), the exact opposite of a shepherd, the divine ideal of a king (cf. 2 Sa 5:2; 7:7; Rev 2:27; 19:15). A hunter gratifies himself at the expense of his victim. By contrast, a shepherd expends himself for the good of the subjects of his care.

Babylonia is called "the land of Nimrod" (Mic 5:6) from the founder of the city-state. He was a Hamite. Upon one branch of the Hamites, there exists a prophetic curse; and in the entire family, there is an absence of divine blessing (Gen 9:25-27).

BABYLON AND THE CONFUSION OF TONGUES

The name *Babylon* is derived by the Hebrews from the root *balal* (to confound). The term perpetuates the story of the colossal pride and rebellion against God that prompted the building of the tower and the consequent judgment of the confusion of languages (Gen 11:9).

The founding of the city in revolt against God and the godless pride of the Babel builders indelibly fixed the character of Babylon in the eyes of the Israelites and all people loyal to the Lord in subsequent generations. Accordingly, Babylon acquired a definite figurative meaning in Bible prophecy.

BABYLON — POLITICAL AND ECCLESIASTICAL

In the prophetic writings — when the actual city in lower Babylonia is not intended — the reference is to the "confusion" that prevails in the satanic world system built on the same principles of pride and rebellion against God as was the ancient city of Nimrod and the tower of Babel built later.

Although this confusion honeycombs all phases of life apart from and lived in rebellion against God, it manifests itself chiefly in the religious sphere (Rev 17) and in the political realm (Rev 18).

Political Babylon is the confusion into which the governmental order of the world has fallen under Gentile world domination (Lk 21:24; Rev 6:14). It began when Judah was carried away to Babylon by Nebuchadnezzar II beginning in 605 B.C. and Jerusalem fell in 586 B.C. At that time, Babylon was at the zenith of its power, greatness, and glory.

The divine order to be realized in the kingdom age is given in Isaiah 11:1 — 12:6. Israel is seen in her own land in fellowship with Christ, as the center of the divine government of the world and the medium of the divine blessing. Gentile nations will appear blessed in association with Israel. Anything else, according to the scriptural view of things, is mere political Babel.

Religious Babylon is the confusion into which the spiritual and ecclesiastical order of the world has fallen as a result of the rejection of the Word of God. Although it culminates in apostate Christendom of the end time, it includes all apostate religions, whether they have any Christian affiliation or not. Ecclesiastical Babylon is prefigured by the "great harlot" (Rev 17:15-18).

WHAT PRICE APOSTASY?

While periodic departure from "the faith which was once for all delivered to the saints" (Jude 3) has characterized all periods of church history, the final age-end apostasy is predicted to eclipse anything that has preceded it. The Spirit of God in most solemn language anticipates it and warns that it will be engineered by seducing spirits. The result would be teachings instigated by demons (1 Ti 4:1).

These seducing spirits are foreseen as operating through false prophets, producing the spiritual confusion that will cause mystical Babylon with its anti-Christian teachings to materialize (1 Jn 4:1-6).

The apostle Peter describes in detail these false teachers who will prepare the way for mystical Babylon (2 Pe 2). The apostle Jude censures them, producing, as they do, the harlot church instead of the true virgin church of Christ (Jude 8-19).

This fearful movement of apostasy, indited and energized by demonic spirits, has been most noticeable since the fundamentalist-modernist controversies of 1920-1934. Since 1934, apostasy and heresy have increased like an avalanche.

Today astrology, fortune-telling, magic, spiritualism, and other elements of demonized religionism are on the increase. The demon-energized aspects of ancient Babylonian religion that had their roots in God-defying idolatry are being revived in modern dress and practiced in witchcraft and various types of sorcery.

The stage is being set before our eyes for the final consummation of mystical Babylon. In the gross spiritual darkness that will engulf the end of this age, the tawdry harlot will appear to sin-blinded eyes as worthy and honorable. But such blindness and deception are the price of abandoning the truth for a lie.

THE ECUMENICAL MANIA

It is significant that the movement for church union in the twentieth century has been largely coeval with the progress of apostasy occasioned by growing unbelief in the full inspiration and authority of Scripture. Between 1910 and 1961, forty-two mergers took place between church bodies in various parts of the world.[1]

In 1925 the ecumenical movement actually began with a series of interchurch conclaves. In 1938 a protem ecumenical council was formed. World War II interrupted progress, but in 1948 the World Council of Churches was founded.[2]

The purpose of this body is to embrace all Christendom by uniting all churches in one superchurch. According to the view of the world council, this is what the Bible teaches. The claim is that this is the only way the church can survive the modern flood tide of secularism.

WHAT'S WRONG WITH ECUMENICALISM?

The danger in this fine-sounding group is that it is not difficult to picture a halo over any movement that professes to bind up the wounds of the Christian church and bring together the disjointed members of Christ's body. Especially is this true when such merging is alleged to be supported by the Scripture and to minister to the health and welfare of the church.

As far as alleged support from the Bible is concerned, the Scriptures most clearly do not advocate a one-church organization. The Bible instead declares that believers in Christ are already one in the body of Christ (Jn 17:20-21; 1 Co 12:12-26). This unity is spiritual, vital, and organic — *not* organizational. It does not preclude believers being members of local churches or groups of local churches. Nor do denominational differences in doctrine or government nullify this essential unity of all true believers.

There are absolutely no biblical directives that require Christians to submit to a superchurch with control from the top. Such an arrangement is clearly an open door to regimentation of doctrine and practice, an obvious peril to be avoided.

The ecumenical movement is fostered largely by Christian leaders who attach little importance to biblical authority and sound doctrine. Their writings and statements often clash with the tenets of orthodox Christianity. Their concept of church union is an example of their weakness in solid Bible doctrine.

ENDING THE SCANDAL OF DIVISION?

When the World Council of Churches was born in a burst of ecumenical euphoria in 1948, the event for many promised to end, once for all, the "scandal of division" that for centuries has cut up Christendom into numerous conflicting and sometimes contending camps.

During its more than two decades of operation, the World Council's achievements in attempting to end this "scandal" have been considerable. Over 252 denominations in 83 countries have been brought into a common fellowship.[3]

No doubt, from the nonbiblical point of view, this accomplishment is considerable and has at least reduced the hint of scandal. However, from the biblical standpoint, the scandal is not really reduced by external organization on the basis of doctrinal laxity and compromise. It is removed by realizing the vital, spiritual unity believers have in union with Christ and counting on that unity. Only then does the oneness Christians have in Christ become manifest in their experience of Christ. In turn, experience of Christ will rise above all denominational barriers and heal the scandal of division by taking in *all Christ's* people, as Christ did.

CREATING NEW SCANDALS?

In abandoning true biblical orientation, the ecumenical World Council of Churches is not only not genuinely solving the problem of division, it faces the peril of losing sight of its rightful task and engaging in activities creating new scandals far more serious than organizational divisions.

An article in the October 1971 issue of *Reader's Digest,* entitled "Must Our Churches Finance Revolution?" exposes some scandalous activities of the World Council of Churches. These include employing church power and church funds to promote insurrection in the United States and Africa, to support avowedly communist groups and American draft dodgers and deserters.[4]

Losing all sense of the Christian's responsibility for peaceful change by preaching the gospel of redemption, the Council has shifted to a non-Christian approach of force, terror, and revolution to effect social goals. What could happen to the ecumenical church is what happened in 1968 to the so-called University Christian Movement. Closing up shop in New York's Interchurch Center, it tacked this notice on the entrance: "Gone out of business. Didn't know what our business was."[5]

CHURCH SURVIVAL IN A SECULAR SOCIETY

Ecumenists frequently bolster their ecumenical dream by calling up the specter of secularism. They reason that the only way the church can survive in an increasingly irreligious society is to unite organizationally.

The "in unity there is strength" principle has become almost a battle cry with ecumenical zealots. Too often, however, the simple fact is overlooked that unity means strength only when those who get together have a common vision and goal. If those who join themselves in outward organization abandon the inward principles and practices that have always formed the core of dynamic biblical Christianity, weakness — not strength — is the inevitable result.

Doctrinal compromise, so characteristic of the modern ecumenical movement, produces spiritual flabbiness incapable of coping with the genuine peril of present-day secularism. Vital biblical

Christianity clashes head on with secularism and triumphs over it by retrieving true believers from its flood.

Emaciated ecumenicalism avoids a clash. Rather, it resorts to compromise and accommodation. The outcome can scarcely be said to be survival. Rather it is capitulation and conformity. The outward "form of godliness" is retained, but the inward "power" renounced (2 Ti 3:5).

This predicted latter-day brand of professing Christianity, which retains the trappings but renounces the power, is the prophesied precursor of mystical Babylon. It prepares the way for the ecclesiastical harlot who will cunningly imitate the true virgin church of Christ.

ECUMENICALISM AND PROPHECY

John F. Walvoord has pointed out the great prophetic significance of the ecumenical movement that has arisen in our day. He shows how this theme forms a vital part of one of the three categories under which practically all Bible prediction falls — the nations, Israel, and the body of Christ.

Prophecy concerning the body of Christ, besides including the hope of rapture, reward, and eternal bliss with Christ, also embraces prediction of the career and fate of the organized church, or Christendom. This includes those who outwardly follow Jesus Christ but are devoid of inner spiritual reality.[6]

The modern ecumenical church to a large degree operates in the sphere of Christendom. Weak in doctrine and biblical orientation, the movement would be expected to appeal mainly to the religious but unregenerate.

FUTURE OF THE ECUMENICAL CHURCH

The future of the ecumenical church is clearly outlined in the Bible. Two great predicted events will dramatically effect it — the rapture of the true church and the judgment of the tribulation period.

The rapture will remove all genuine believers from the ranks of the ecumenical church, and this group will then be swallowed up in the demonic delusion that will then cover the earth. This awesome prediction is solemnly made in one of the most astonishing prophetic passages in the New Testament. It is recorded in 2 Thessalonians chapter 2.

The apostle Paul presents the truth that the rapture of the church will take place *before* the day of the Lord (the tribulation) and the awful apostasy and demon delusion that will settle like an impenetrable fog upon the earth (2 Th 2:1-9).

After the rapture, it is predicted that those left behind in the ranks of the professing church, who did not receive "the love of the truth that they might be saved," will come under divine judgment. God will turn them over to demonic forces to completely delude them.

The deception of those who rejected and opposed the truth of God's Word will be so thoroughgoing that they will believe "*the* lie," the personal Antichrist (Jn 5:43; 2 Th 2:10-11; Rev 13:8, 16-18).

The delusion is sent so that all in the ecumenical church might be judged and found guilty for not having cherished and believed the Word of God during the church age. The penalty will be physical death for millions in the judgments of the tribulation period. Other millions will be deluded and tormented short of death by myriads of vile and vicious demons let loose from the abyss (Rev 9:1-12).

Demon-deluded truth rejecters will be helplessly and hopelessly sucked into the maelstrom of age-end demonized religion (Rev 9:20-21).

Occult Revival and Demonized Religion

The precursor to this awful condition is the cult of the occult that is coming to the fore in the age of Aquarius. When men depart from God's Word, they expose themselves to the operation of demon powers. The result is "doctrines of devils [demons]" (1 Ti 4:1). These demonic teachings imbue liberalism and neoorthodoxy, that set aside the Word of God, as well as the cults of Christianity that profess to honor it.

But insofar as the sects and cults of Christianity are concerned, to the degree they deny or distort the Word by ignorance or otherwise, they expose themselves to demon powers and doctrines of demons. The result is religion that is demonized to the extent that evil powers gain entrance through failure on the part of God's people to stand solidly on the ground of biblical truth.

Enter — the Harlot Church

Revelation 17 presents in symbolic form the future development of the ecumenical church. This is not the present ecumenical movement. It is rather the portrayal of the world church after the rapture, with every true believer removed. It is prepared for gross demonic delusion and ripe for judgment.

How fitting that this wicked religious system should be presented as a lewd harlot riding into power on the political system, pictured as a scarlet-colored beast.

The beast is full of names of blasphemy. It has "seven heads" and "ten horns." In Revelation 13 this beast is presented as the revived Roman empire, presided over by the Antichrist. The woman rides into power on the beast. Moreover she is in a dominant position where she can direct the beast (Rev 17:3).

Clearly Scripture predicts an alliance between the future apostate church and the last-day, world political power. Together they will connive to tighten their control over the world.

As a harlot, the woman will have renounced every semblance to the pure virgin church of Christ. She will be the devil's imitation. All her tawdry external finery, procured through ill-gotten gain and base compromise of God's truth, will not be able to hide the wickedness and adultery of her heart.

Murderess of the True Followers of Jesus

The "golden cup" filled with "abominations" are the idolatrous doctrines and practices the harlot has followed that have plunged her into corrupt, demonized religionism. The "filthiness of her fornication" reveals her gross infidelity to God and His Word (Rev 17:4-5).

In the end-time persecution, this evil system personifying religious revolt against God, in its final form ripened for judgment, will participate with the beast in the wholesale murder of the true followers of Jesus (Rev 17:6).

DESTRUCTON OF THE HARLOT

At the moment the harlot is apparently triumphant, God's judgment falls upon her. Amazingly, God's Word predicts her destruction (Rev 17:16-17). This will come at the hand of the God-defying political system the harlot so shamelessly used to ride into power.

The harlot's destroyers are the ten kings (Rev 17:12) who are associated with the beast (Antichrist), the head of the revived Roman empire (Rev 13:7). The Antichrist and the ten confederated kings will turn against the harlot. They will hate her and utterly desolate her. God will cause them to do this and to give their kingdom to the beast to fulfill God's Word.

SATAN'S MASTERPIECE — THE FINAL WORLD RELIGION

When the harlot church is destroyed at the pinnacle of its power, it will be replaced by the final world religion. This substitute for Christianity will be completely satanic and will represent total religious revolt against God and the divine program for the earth.

Satan's program is one of imitation and substitution. The dragon (Satan) will simulate God the Father. The beast (world ruler) will parallel Jesus Christ as absolute king and lord over the earth. The false prophet will mimic the Holy Spirit. He will cause men to worship the beast (world ruler) and the Antichrist (Rev 13:11-18).

He "shall do according to his will; and he shall exalt himself, and magnify himself above every god" (Dan 11:36). He will exalt himself above the one true God and sit in the restored Jewish temple in Jerusalem, claiming to be God and demanding worship of the whole world (Dan 11:36-45, 2 Th 2:4).

GOAL OF SATAN'S RELIGION

The Antichrist will worship "the god of fortresses" (Dan 11:38). He will be a thoroughgoing materialist. He will own no god but military power. He will give his precious things in order to build up military strength.

His purpose will be to banish the name of God and frustrate God's plan for the earth centering in Christ and the nation Israel. Hence he must destroy the Jew and take over the earth in His own name, in opposition to Christ's name and claim over this globe by virtue of creation and redemption.

Satan's religion will accordingly have its purpose in destroying all enemies, taking over the earth, and usurping God's place of sovereignty and power through Satan's man, the Antichrist.

To accomplish his dream, Satan will employ his masterpiece of religion to furnish the dynamic for Armageddon, his war of extermination of everything standing in the way of his take-over of the earth.

COMMUNISM AND SATAN'S RELIGION

One of the most startling developments of the twentieth century has been the rise and rapid spread of atheistic, materialistic Communism. Although principally a political ideology that opposes all religions, strong demonic impress and dynamic give Communism sinister religious overtones.

In its religious aspect, Communism is teaching tens of millions of youth that there is no God, except the god of materialism and military might. Startlingly enough, this is exactly what Daniel predicted concerning the Antichrist of the last days in his honoring the "god of fortresses," that is, the power of military might (Dan 11:38).

Just as the ecumenical church of the present time is laying the groundwork for the apostate world church after the rapture of the true church of Christ, so Communism is preparing the way for that form of atheism which will finalize in Satan's world religion. This delusion will capture the minds of men as they worship this world's ruler and find in him the solution to their problems.

SATAN'S RELIGION AND THE FOLLY OF ARMAGEDDON

Being completely satanic, the final world religion will enjoy complete demonic dynamic. This is why its take-over will be rapid and thoroughgoing after the destruction of the harlot church. It will be abetted by an upsurge of diabolic miracle and supernatural deception absolutely unprecedented in the history of the world (2 Th 2:8-12; Rev 13:1-18).

"Many false prophets shall rise, and shall deceive many" (Mt 24:11). They "shall shew great signs and wonders; insomuch that, if it were possible, they shall deceive the very elect" (Mt 24:24).

The same demons that energize Satan's religion energize his plan to take over the earth. "Unclean spirits like frogs come out of the mouth of the dragon, and out of the mouth of the beast, and out of the mouth of the false prophet. For they are the spirits of devils, working miracles, which go forth unto the kings of the earth and of the whole world, to gather them to the battle of that great day of God Almighty" (Rev 16:13-14).

Though the demons gather wicked men to Armageddon for the supreme folly of fighting against God, it is really the omnipotent and sovereign God who gathers *them,* employing the demons as instruments of His punishment of rebellious men. "And he [God] gathered them together into a place called . . . Armageddon" (Rev 16:16).

CRASH OF THE SATANIC WORLD SYSTEM

The destruction of the Antichrist and his armies at Armageddon will be effected by the victorious Christ returning from heaven with His armies and saints to slay His foes and set up His kingdom. Satan and his demons will be shut up in the abyss (Zec 13:2; Rev 20:1-3). The beast and the false prophet will be cast alive into the lake of fire (Rev 19:20; 20:10), and earth's rebels will be crushed in death.

With Satan, the beast, and the false prophet removed from the scene, the satanic world system, in all its aspects, religious, political, and commercial, will collapse, making way for Christ's reign on the earth.

EXIT RELIGIOUS CONFUSION

The destruction of the harlot church and the complete overthrow of Satan and his program of delusion and violence to take over the earth will spell the end of mystical Babylon.

At last "the mother of harlots and of the abominations of the earth" (Rev 17:5) will have come to her predestined end. With her fall, religious confusion will be banished from the earth, as Christ takes His rightful place as "King of kings, and Lord of lords" (Rev 19:16).

4

Millions Vanish in a Moment

MODERN MAN is becoming accustomed to breathtaking marvels. In our day, before our very eyes, God is permitting humanity to achieve feats in the natural realm bordering on the miraculous. Man, relentlessly subduing the earth, is pressing on into planetary space, determined to conquer the universe and to set his "nest among the stars" (Ob 4).

When Apollo 11 landed on the moon, it was as if God was saying to an awestricken world: "You are astounded that the astronauts are walking on the moon? Be much more astounded. The time is drawing near when I will take millions on a far greater trip into space. But no launching pad or nuclear power will be needed. No spaceship nor space suit will be required. My power shall raise from death those who have died in the Lord, and immortalize the bodies of those who are in Christ and living at the time. I will equip My own to live in space but beyond time and above space in the wonderful realm above the natural world."

WONDER OF WONDERS

Of all the events that loom up on the horizon of biblical prophecy, none is more incredibly stupendous than the predicted translation of the true church of Jesus Christ.

Our Lord spoke of this dramatically glorious event that will drastically change the course of human history. "In my Father's house are many mansions: if it were not so, I would have told you. I go to prepare a place for you. And if I go and prepare a place for you, I will come again, and receive you unto myself; that where I am, there ye may be also" (Jn 14:2-3).

Imagine! "The Lord himself shall descend from heaven." Hear his shout of triumph over death (1 Co 15:54-57), as He raises the dead saints and instantly glorifies the living saints.

Hear the voice of the archangel Michael, who is associated with resurrection (Dan 12:1-2), as it blends with the shout of the death-conquering Christ and merges with the trumpet of God summoning the saints heavenward.

What a scene! The dead in Christ rise *first*. Then in an instant, the saints who are living when the Lord comes "shall be caught up" in "the clouds" to meet the Lord in the air (1 Th 4:13-18).

Why Call It "Rapture"?

We refer to this sudden homegoing of all the saints as the "rapture" because the Scripture says the living glorified saints together with the saints resurrected from their graves will be "caught up" to meet the Lord in the air. The Greek verb *harpageomai* means to snatch away suddenly, take away forcefully, to seize or claim for oneself.[1] In the New Testament it always expresses the operation of the mighty power of God.[2]

The apostle Paul was "caught up" in vision to the third heaven (2 Co 12:2, 4). The Spirit of the Lord suddenly "caught away" the apostle Philip and transported him miraculously to Azotus, some miles distant (Ac 8:39-40). The male Child, Christ, whom the woman, Israel, bears is "caught up" in vision to God's throne (Rev 12:5).

Accordingly, the term *rapture* refers to the act or the event of carrying away or being suddenly transported to another sphere, either in the actual body or in spirit in a vision. The term aptly describes what will happen when Christ returns for His own. However, the word *rapture* in the noun form does not actually occur in the Bible.

WHY NOT CALL IT "TRANSLATION"?

Many people refer to this great event of the removal of the church as "translation" rather than the "rapture." The former term has the advantage of actually occurring in the Bible. Enoch was "translated that he should not see death." "Before his translation he had this testimony, that he pleased God" (Heb 11:5).

Translation, accordingly, is the change from one place, position, or condition to another, specifically a transference to heaven without the experience of physical death. The thought emphasizes that aspect of the removal of the true church of God which underscores the transformation that will take place in believers when Christ comes for them. Accordingly, the terms *translation* and *rapture* represent two sides of the same coin.

Translation underscores the apostle's description given to the Corinthian believers, as *rapture* features his account to the Thessalonians. His words to the former set forth the incredible thrill this stupendous event holds in store for all believers: "We shall not all sleep [die], but we shall all be changed, in a moment, in the twinkling of an eye, at the last trump; for the trumpet shall sound, and the dead shall be raised incorruptible, and we shall be changed" (1 Co 15:51-52).

CONQUEST OF TIME AND SPACE

When the great transformation takes place, those in Christ will receive a new body. What a glorious body! Like the resurrection body of Christ that came forth from the empty tomb through the solid rock! The stone was not rolled away to let the risen Saviour out; it was rolled away by angelic power to show mankind that the tomb was already empty! The body of the risen Christ came through the solid rock!

The empty tomb and the risen Saviour are the guarantee that the believer will receive a new body — a body adapted to a new sphere under the laws of the spiritual realm.

No longer will this new body be subject to decay and death. No longer will it be afflicted with infirmity, sin, or sickness. No longer will it be confined to natural law or limited by time and space.

What the astronauts have accomplished after years of research and preparation, believers with a glorified body will be able to do instantly. Nor will they need space capsules and space suits, nor atomic energy to propel them. God's power released through the glorified body will accomplish all this in the twinkling of an eye.

MILLIONS THEN LIVING WILL NEVER DIE

But the greatest triumph of all at the rapture will be the conquest of death. No believer living when Christ returns for His own will ever die!

"So when this corruptible shall have put on incorruption, and this mortal shall have put on immortality, then shall be brought to pass the saying that is written, Death is swallowed up in victory. O death, where is thy sting? O grave, where is thy victory?" (1 Co 15:54-55).

DIVINE TRUTH OR DOWNRIGHT DRIVEL?

Many shake their heads in disbelief. Others indignantly protest: "Such an event is impossible." "Pure ridiculous nonsense!" "Pious drivel!"

Millions of people vanishing in an instant? What will happen to the jet streaking through the air like lightning, with one or more of its pilots gone? What will be the fate of the locomotive hurtling down the track, with the engineer vanishing into thin air? What will be the result on the crowded expressways when numbers of motorists suddenly disappear from behind the wheel? What about the legal tangles that will develop when wills are invalidated as people vanish but leave no proof of death, because they did not die?

These are questions for the unsaved who are left to wrestle with. They did not receive "the love of the truth" when it was available that they might be saved (2 Th 2:10). Hence their unregenerate, natural minds will not be able to comprehend the truth of God (1 Co 2:14). It will be foolishness to them. To them the idea of the rapture will be an uproarious joke! Besides, God will judicially expose them to gross deception after the rapture has taken place. They would not believe the truth concerning Christ; therefore, they will fall for the lie of the Antichrist (2 Th 2:11-12).

For unbelievers, the rapture will be awesome, in that it will separate them from believers and seal them in their doom.

For believers the event will be thrilling and unimaginably glorious. For unbelievers it will introduce the time of worldwide confusion, deception, and judgment that will wind up the last awful years of this present age (2 Th 2:11-12). The prophetic Word describes this period as "the great tribulation" (cf. Jer 30:5-7; Mt 24:3-28; Rev 7:14).

Behold, a Mystery

The apostle Paul tells us why the idea of the rapture is ludicrous to unbelievers and why it is well-nigh incredible even to some Christians. It is a "mystery" (1 Co 15:51), not something unrevealed, but something revealed; it is a secret, to be sure, which has always been in God's plan, but which has not been made known to His own until a certain point in time.

But what truth does Paul refer to as a mystery regarding the rapture of the church, that was not previously made known but is now revealed? It is the fact that not everyone will die. Those believers who are living when Christ returns for His own will never experience physical death!

The astonishing aspect of the rapture is the mystery part. That men would be raised from the dead was not a mystery. It was clearly declared and taught in the Old Testament (Job 19:25; Is 26:19; Dan 12:2). Christ taught the same truth (Jn 5:26-29), as did the apostle Paul (1 Co 15:1-49).

But no hint had been given until the apostle's revelation of the mystery of the translation of the church that anyone could enter into God's presence apart from death and resurrection.

To be sure, Enoch and Elijah had both been translated (given glorified bodies without experiencing death). But there was no promise that anyone else would experience what they did.

For this reason the newly revealed promise, "We shall not all sleep [die]" is called a *mystery*.

New Route to God's Presence

The mystery involved in the translation of the church at the rapture discloses a new route to heaven. The dead saints will go via resurrection. But the living saints will go by way of translation (1 Co 15:52).

In either case, God's power will effect the necessary change when the Lord Jesus comes. The dead in Christ, of course, have experienced the corruption of death. They will therefore put on incorruption when the body is resurrected.

But those who are living when the Lord descends for His own will not have experienced death. They will not have seen corruption. They will undergo a different kind of change. Being mortal, they will simply be clothed with immortality.

Having never tasted physical death, how grand will be their cry of victory over the grave (1 Co 15:54-55).

What About a "Partial Rapture"?

Some contend that only certain believers will be raptured. Others are seen left behind to go through a purifying process in the time of trouble that follows the rapture.

However, Scripture seems to clearly teach a total rapture involving *all* true believers living on the earth when the Lord comes back.

Paul declares we shall "all be changed." He also specifies clearly the time of the change. He says it will occur "in a moment, in the twinking of an eye" (1 Co 15:52).

The whole stupendous transaction, the resurrection of the dead in Christ and the translation of the living saints, will be instantaneous, not gradual. The Greek word rendered "moment" (*atomos*) means uncut or indivisible because of smallness, and here has reference to an indivisible instant of time in which the rapture will take place.

The instantaneous nature of the rapture is also emphasized by the phrase "in the twinkling of an eye." The Greek word rendered "twinkling" meaning a rapid sweep, a jerk, or twitch, apparently refers either to the momentary casting of a glance or the rapid movement seen in the involuntary split-second blinking of the eyelids.[3]

The phrase "at the last trump" reminds us of the finality of the event. "After the trumpet sounds, there will be no time to prepare, for the change will occur instantly. There will be no second chance for those who, up till then, have refused the grace of God."[4] (This refers to those in the professing church who heard the gospel and rejected it or resisted the proclamation.) The "last trump" is evidently to be connected with the silver trumpets used in the wilderness wanderings. They were blown to call together the assembly. When the last trumpet blast was sounded, it was the symbol to move on to another place (Num 10:1-10).

It may be concluded then that the rapture will be instantaneous and final. It will clearly include *all* believers, not simply some of them.

What About a "Secret Rapture"?

People frequently speak of a "secret rapture," but this concept is misleading. This is true, despite the fact that not the event itself but only its effects will be observed by unbelievers.

The rapture will be an event for the Lord's people. It constitutes their "blessed hope" (Titus 2:11-13). The Lord comes for them, not for the world. He consequently does not come to the earth, but descends from heaven to meet His own caught up "in the clouds" to meet Him "in the air" (1 Th 4:17).

Accordingly, the event itself will not be *seen* by the world. Only its effects will be observed. But these will be public and known by everybody in all areas where true believers were before it occurs. In many instances, what happens will be horrifying.

A man riding in a bus or plane sees the person in the seat beside him suddenly vanish. A pilot and copilot both disappear from the cockpit of the jet, while the plane dives through space to crash eventually in a fiery explosion, killing all aboard.

A group of ultraliberal churchmen on their way to an ecumenical conclave are horrified to see the driver of the airport limousine, in which they are passengers, suddenly disappear while the vehicle wildly careens for a head-on crash on the open freeway.

Godless husbands who harassed their Christian wives will see them disappear forever as they talk to them. Rebellious teenagers who despised their Christian parents, will find at last they are "free" of parental restraint, as both father and mother are nowhere to be found.

Hardly a "secret rapture"!

Hard Pressed to Explain What Happened

Such an unprecendented disappearance of so many people will tax the ingenuity of those left behind for a rational explanation. Unregenerate men in all walks of life will rack their brains to explain away what they are utterly unable to explain rationally and reasonably.

The professor of the philosophy of religion in a liberal seminary

"These people who have so mysteriously disappeared, so far as I have been able to determine, were blind obscurantists who refused to subscribe to the findings of higher criticism of the Bible. Stubbornly they maintained faith in the Bible as the 'inspired' and 'authoritative' Word of God. I had two of them in my class. Continually they challenged my conclusions by reference to Scripture. Academically, I would say, good riddance. But I'm at a loss to really explain their disappearance."

Pastor of an ecumenical church

"My dear friends, I know it is hard to have loved ones disappear so suddenly. But we can console ourselves that those who have gone were most trying. Their narrow fundamental stand for the sole authority of the Bible led them to oppose the great advances of the church in our day. Continually they thwarted our noble efforts to unite humanity under the banner of the Fatherhood of God and the brotherhood of all men, irrespective of creed or religious affiliation. We may explain their disappearance as divine judgment against bigotry and narrow, religious provincialism."

GODLESS POLITICIAN

"Now with these fanatics for morality and decency gone, we can really advance interests that will feather our political nest and give us powers from criminal elements and the underworld."

COMMUNIST SUBVERSIVE

"What a boon to our program to advance atheistic materialism and plan governmental take-over! Those that are gone were the real champions of liberty and a free society. Christians have always been our chiefest foes in our program of enslaving the human family. Now at last we are rid of them!"

DEBATING THE WHEN OF THE RAPTURE

It is singular indeed that the time when such a tremendous event as the rapture will occur is subject to wide differences of opinion among sincere Christians. Some place it before the tribulation. Some locate it in the middle of the tribulation. Some pinpoint it at the end of the tribulation and equate it with Christ's second advent.

Personally, I believe the rapture will occur *before* the tribulation. Hence it is to be clearly differentiated from the second advent. In the light of honest divergence of opinion on the point, let us adduce the principal reasons for our position.

In 2 Thessalonians 2:1-12, the apostle Paul argues for the pretribulation rapture against mid- or posttribulation views. He plainly states our gathering together to the Lord (v. 1) will occur before the day of the Lord (the tribulation). His reference to the Restrainer being taken out of the way (v. 7) finds its only adequate explanation in the departure of the Holy Spirit in the glorified church in the same sense He came to form that body at Pentecost.

Our Lord promised to keep the Philadelphian church out of the worldwide tribulation, meaning both the event as well as the time in which it occurs (Rev. 3:10). He gives the pretribulation rapture promise to this church because it represents the great bulk of regenerated believers in the world when the rapture occurs.

Believers are promised deliverance from the wrath of God in

the coming tribulation (1 Th 5:2, 9; cf. Rev 6:17). In the book of the Revelation, after the church period (Rev 2-3), the church appears in heaven, but not on earth (Rev 4:1 — 19:10). It remains in heaven until it returns with Christ in glory at His second advent (Rev 19:11-16).

THE RAPTURE VERSUS THE REVELATION OF CHRIST

The rapture and the revelation of Christ, it seems to me, can scarcely be equated with Christ's coming in glory and assumed to be simultaneous with it.

The rapture is private in the sense that Christ comes only for His own. He resurrects or translates them to take them to heaven to reward them. As an event it is seen by no one on earth. All earthlings see is the *effect* of the event.

The revelation is public. It is seen by every eye. Christ comes in power and glory to slay His enemies and set up His kingdom (Rev 1:7; 19:11-16). He comes *with* His own, not *for* them. They come, having already been rewarded, not to be rewarded.

At the rapture, Christ comes in the outer atmosphere, not to the earth. Saints are caught up to meet Him in the air (1 Th 4:13-18). His feet do not touch the earth.

At the revelation, Christ comes to the earth. His feet stand on Mount Olivet (Zec 14:4; Ac 1:10-12).[5] Saints are not caught up to meet Him, but accompany Him to share His victory and glory.

THE RAPTURE AND CHRIST'S KINGDOM

When Christ comes in His glorious second advent, He will judge the nations (Mt 25:31-46). He will separate the sheep and the goats among the Gentiles. This judgment will be a necessary prelude to the establishment of the kingdom. The sheep represent "those among the Gentiles who have come to Christ during the awful time of tribulation after the rapture."[6] The goats represent those who remain unsaved and godless during this period of worldwide trouble.

"Now if the Rapture were to take place at the same time as the second coming, how could believers and unbelievers be separated on earth?"[7] There would be no believers on earth to be separated from unbelievers, because all living believers will be caught up to join Christ in heaven at the rapture.

Moreover, the predicted kingdom which Christ will set up when He returns to earth will have mortal, unglorified humanity in it. If the rapture occurred at the second advent, there would be no unglorified humanity who would be believers. Hence there would be no one to enter into the kingdom to repopulate the millennial earth.[8]

THE RAPTURE AND ITS IMMINENCE

Is the coming of the Lord for His own imminent? May it occur today? Or does some prophecy or event have to transpire first?

This is the question that troubled the Thessalonian saints. They had lost the sense of imminence and the truth of the pretribulation rapture. They imagined that the troubles of the day of the Lord were already upon them. Paul wrote to restore them to the confidence that Christ's coming for His own was always to be regarded as impending, with the possibility of occurring at any time and without delay (2 Th 2:1-8).

The apostle pointed out that the rapture or "gathering together" to the Lord of His saints (v. 1) did not depend upon the day of the Lord coming first, or the development of the apostasy, or the building of the tribulation temple in Jerusalem, or the rise of the Antichrist and satanic delusion, or any other development.

The rapture of the church, so far as God has revealed in His Word, the apostle would show, has *always* been imminent. As far as any predicted event standing in the way of its occurrence, there was none in apostolic days. There is none now.

Jesus may come today!

But if the rapture will not occur until the middle of the tribulation or at the end of it, Jesus may *not* come today. His coming is not imminent, and the events the apostle employed to correct the wrong views of the Thessalonians must then first take place before the rapture occurs.

The Rapture and the Blessed Hope

The Lord's coming for His own constitutes the "blessed hope" the Christian has to look forward to (Titus 2:13). The word *blessed* means happy. The hope is "happy" because it fills the believer with joyful expectation. And little wonder! What a prospect to receive a glorified body if one is living when Christ comes for His own or to be raised from the dead, if one has already died. In either case, the result will be instant glory for the believer!

But the full blessedness of the hope is not realized apart from the truth of the imminence of Christ's return for His own. It is the hope of being alive when Christ comes and never experiencing physical death that anticipates the full thrill of the Christian hope.

This is why the New Testament has held out the blessed hope to every generation of Christians. Every believer who has this hope ablaze in his heart "purifieth himself, even as he is pure" (1 Jn 3:3).

In every way the blessed hope has great practical value for God's people. It inspires them as nothing else can, to be "steadfast, unmoveable, always abounding in the work of the Lord." This is true because the believer, in the light of future resurrection or translation at the Lord's coming, knows that his "labor is not in vain in the Lord" (1 Co 15:58).

Putting First Things First

The study of the prophetic Word in showing us what lies ahead, prepares us to live meaningfully and wisely in the present. The coming of the Lord and "the blessed hope" centered in Him teach and discipline us not only negatively to deny "ungodliness and worldly lusts," but positively to "live soberly, righteously, and godly, in this present world" (Titus 2:12-13).

Only as we live day by day in the light of the Lord's soon coming and our gathering together unto Him, will we give top priority to the things that are spiritual, and hence eternal and of paramount importance.

"When we meet Christ face to face, we're going to look back on this life and see that the things we thought were important here were like the discarded toys of our childhood."[9]

Occupation with Christ alone will arrest the mad folly of chasing after the proverbial pot of gold at the end of the rainbow, as millions of worldlings caught in the whirlpool of secularism and materialism are doing today.

Looking for and awaiting Christ's coming will break the spell that selfish pleasure and self-indulgence are casting upon us.

The apostle's exhortation and prayer are timely in our evil day: "If anyone does not love the Lord, let him be accursed. Our Lord, come!" (1 Co 16:22, author's trans. of the Greek).

5

The Saints Rewarded in Glory

THE TRANSLATION OF BELIEVERS who are living when Christ returns and the resurrection of those who have died in the Lord furnish the glorious prelude to thrilling experiences that take place in heaven for God's people. While divine judgments are being poured out upon the earth, the saints will be in heaven with the Lord.

Two major events, which every child of God may joyfully anticipate, are outlined in the prophetic Word and will occur in the celestial realms after the rapture. The first is the judgment of the believer's works with the dispensing of rewards. The second is the public identification of Christ with His glorified people, prefigured as His marriage to them.

SAINTS WILL BE JUDGED!

Among the revelations concerning the future, of particular significance to Christians is that concerning the judgment seat of Christ. Stephen F. Olford calls this subject "an intensely solemn and searching aspect of prophetic truth."[1]

Addressing the saints at Corinth, the apostle Paul by prophetic inspiration declared that "all" believers would one day have to stand before this special tribunal "that each one may be recompensed for his deeds in the body, according to what he has done, whether good or bad" (2 Co 5:10, NASB).

As Henry Varley said, this judgment "has reference to the members of the body of Christ *only*."[2] It is a distinctive adjudication for

55

a unique group, those saved between Pentecost and the rapture of the church, consisting of those baptized by one Spirit into the body of Christ, the church (1 Co 12:13) and constituted saints.

The frequent and consistent use of the pronoun *we* in the context of 2 Corinthians 5, can have reference only to believers (saints). The same fact is true of the context of Romans 14:8-10, the other great passage dealing with the believer's judgment: "For if we live, we live for the Lord, or if we die, we die for the Lord; therefore whether we live or die, we are the Lord's. For to this end Christ died and lived again, that He might be Lord both of the dead and of the living. But you, why do you judge your brother? Or you again, why do you regard your brother with contempt? For we shall all stand before the judgment-seat of God" (NASB).

However, if only believers appear, yet *all* believers will appear. Not one of them will be absent. "We shall *all* stand" (Ro 14:10). "We must *all* appear" (2 Co 5:10). Not one saint, no matter how carnal or unfaithful, is excluded. Even the apostles and martyrs, as well as the humblest and most obscure believer, will be judged for actions in this life, since becoming a Christian.

WILL SINNERS BE JUDGED WITH SAINTS?

Though *all* saints will appear at the judgment seat of Christ, not one sinner will be present. This important fact has often been lost sight of, because this pivotal event has frequently been confused with the idea of a general judgment. Under this view, all mankind, saved as well as unsaved, is thought of as appearing before God at the same time to be judged.*

But such a concept as a general judgment cannot be substantiated by a careful study of God's Word. It is the result of failing to discern the divine plan and purpose as revealed in the whole body of truth. As a result, a few seemingly contrary passages, such as Daniel 2:2-3; Matthew 25:31-46; and John 5:28-29 are interpreted in a contextual vacuum and made to teach a general judgment. But

---

* This is largely the view of Lutheran and Reformed theology. Unfortunately the Reformation did not "reform" prophecy and eschatology. It largely confined itself to soteriology, the doctrine of salvation.

Daniel 12:2-3 describes the resurrection of saved Israelites (not church saints) at the end of the tribulation. Unsaved Israelites, like unsaved mankind in general, will not be raised until the second resurrection (Rev. 20:11-15).

John 5:28-29 declares that "all" in their graves (representing saved and unsaved) will be resurrected. But it does not declare, as is sometimes assumed, that both of these classes will hear Christ's voice at the same time and be raised simultaneously. Other Scriptures plainly teach that the first resurrection for the saved is in various stages and separated by a long interval of at least a thousand years from the second resurrection, which is for the unsaved (Lk 14:14; 20:35-36; Rev 20:4-6).

Matthew 25:31-46 portrays not a general judgment but the judgment of the nations living at the second advent of Christ and the establishment of the millennial kingdom. The "sheep" are individuals who receive the gospel of the kingdom (Mt 24:14) and manifest their regenerate state by their kind treatment of the believing remnant of Jews saved during the tribulation (Mt 25:34-36). The "goats" are the unregenerate who reject the gospel of the kingdom and evidence their unsaved condition by persecuting the Jewish remnant (Mt 25:41-46). They will be sentenced to death and thus excluded from the kingdom, sharing the fate of all the unsaved in Gehenna (hell).

Christ Will Be the Judge

Since Christ will preside, this inquest is called "the judgment-seat of Christ" (2 Co 5:10). Because the Father "has given all judgment to the Son" (Jn 5:22, NASB), it is also designated "the judgment-seat of God" (Ro 14:10).

That Christ is the Judge is specifically stated. "Therefore do not go on passing judgment before the time, but wait until the Lord comes who will both bring to light the things hidden in the darkness and disclose the motives of men's hearts; and then each man's praise will come to him from God" (1 Co 4:5, NASB).

The apostle Paul declares, "He that judgeth me is the Lord" (1 Co 4:4).

WHY MUST SAINTS BE JUDGED?

Scripture emphasizes the necessity of the believer's judgment. "For we *must* all be made manifest before the judgment-seat of Christ" (2 Co 5:10). Why the "must"? Because from the divine side, God is who He is and does what He does, and from the human side the believer is who he is and acts the way he does.

God is infinitely righteous and impartial. He must judge all men according to their works. Salvation is solely on the basis of grace through faith — a divine gift totally apart from human works and self-effort (Eph 2:8-9). God *must* judge believers for services rendered after salvation. This is true because Christians differ radically in holiness of conduct and faithfulness in service. God could not maintain His infinitely holy character unless He took this into account.

Accordingly, when appearing before the judgment seat of Christ, the saved are not seen in judgment in any judicial sense (Ro 5:1; 8:1). The trial of their works does not in any manner determine whether they are saved or lost. It strictly determines the reward or forfeiture of reward for service, which will be righteously and impartially meted out to each believer.

Those who stand in this judgment scene will have already been glorified (1 Co 15:51-52; 1 Th 4:16-17). They will be not only saved and safe, but already resurrected or, if living, translated to heaven (1 Jn 3:2). This will have been accomplished, moreover, not on the basis of any human merit or work whatsoever, but solely on the ground of divine grace revealed through Christ.

In the light of God's character and the nature of His gracious salvation, how incongruous to intrude the believer into a so-called general judgment with the unsaved. Since the believer's life and service can in no wise condition his eternal salvation, only a separate judgment, unrelated to that of the unsaved, can at all meet the facts as presented in the Scripture.

SAINTS WILL BE VINDICATED

The world is no friend of grace or of believers. With relentless rage, the serpent's seed (Gen 3:15) has been arrayed against the saints (Rev 12:10-11). Our blessed Saviour, the sinless Son of God, was crucified as a common criminal. Stephen, a "man full of faith and of the Holy Spirit (Ac 6:5), was stoned to death as an impious blasphemer. Paul, the great herald of the cross, was judged a person not fit to live (Ac 22:22).

Early believers were cast to the wild beasts or lighted as human torches to illuminate Nero's garden parties. Millions were sent to death by pagan Rome and by misguided religious zealots during the Dark Ages. Saints throughout the centuries have been accounted as the filth and offscouring of the world (1 Co 4:13).

Will there be no just tribunal to reverse these outrageous decisions? Will there be no divine court to vindicate these of "whom the world was not worthy"? The saints deserve a better judgment. They shall have it! But not in the courts of this world!

At the judgment seat of Christ, the saints will be manifested in their true grandeur. They will appear in their real light and worth. Not only will they be vindicated against their persecutors, but they will be endowed with judicial power to judge the fallen angels (1 Co 6:2-3).

Moreover, at the judgment seat of Christ, vindication will extend to difficulties and inequalities among the saints as well. How often believers have suffered wrongfully at the hands of fellow believers. How often has the humble, loving Christian endured meekly under provocation from a proud, carnal fellow believer. How many injustices have believers perpetrated against other believers in the body of Christ. At the judgment seat of Christ, each believer will be shown in his true light and vindicated of any wrong.

Not until the tribunal at which the saints are judged will "the things hidden in the darkness" be revealed and "the motives of men's hearts" be laid bare. Only "then each man's praise will come to him from God" (1 Co 4:5, NASB).

Saints Will Be Rewarded

Rewarding the faithful for service is the chief purpose of the judgment that will take place before Christ's tribunal. The sphere in which the believer appears is that of a servant. His life and all his actions as a worker for Christ will then come under divine scrutiny. The result will be reward or loss of reward.

Scripture is transparently clear that all believers are saints and have the same position in union with Christ. When the blood-bought throng stands before the Judge, one question will prevail: *How* has each one served his Saviour and Lord?

Scripture very definitely states the purpose of the believer's judgment as a reward for service. "For we must all appear before the judgment-seat of Christ, that each one may be recompensed for his deeds in the body, according to what he has done, whether good or bad" (2 Co 5:10, NASB).

The word *appear* (*phaneroothenai*) means to be made manifest, be revealed in true character. The very character of each Christian's life and service will be laid bare under the unerring and omniscient vision of Christ, whose "eyes [are] as a flame of fire" (Rev 1:14).

Each believer will be "recompensed," or rewarded, "for his deeds" both in his redeemed physical body, as well as in the body of Christ, the church, "according to what he has done." The emphasis is obviously on the believer's works or service.

For the "good" there will be proper reward. For the "bad" (worthless), there will be loss of reward. Saints too often are willing to hear about being recompensed for the good things they have done, but they are prone to overlook the fact that there will also be an accounting for the deeds that are bad and useless as well. "Therefore knowing the fear of the Lord," the apostle Paul warns, "we persuade men" (2 Co 5:11). He pleads with believers to be faithful and diligent, since all their earthly actions and conduct will be subject to Christ's all-seeing search.

Considering our liability to err, "with fear and trembling" (emphatic in the Greek), we are constantly to "work out our salvation" (Phil 2:12). Solemn warning (2 Co 5:11) is added to the apostle's account of the believer's judgment (2 Co 5:10) to stir up Christians to maintain a consistent life of good works.

GOD'S GARDEN — NOT THE DEVIL'S WEED PATCH

In a passage in which the subject of Christian service and reward is amplified, the apostle uses the figure of a cultivated field or garden to describe the believer's life of fruitful service. "For we are God's fellow-workers; you are God's field" (1 Co 3:9). The Greek word *field* (*georgos*) denotes a carefully cultivated piece of ground, such as a farm or garden.

When a soul is saved, God's Spirit begins to convert the devil's weed patch of briers and thorns into a well-ordered orchard. This great work is God's. But it is the result on the human plane of the believer's cooperation with God as "God's fellow-worker."

At the judgment seat of Christ, each believer will be judged according to the degree to which he has cooperated with God in allowing the Spirit of God to refine and sanctify his life, making it conformable to Christ.

Scripture declares that in this process, "He who plants and he who waters are one" because they are fellow workers with God and that "each will receive his own reward according to his own labor" (1 Co 3:8).

Facing the Test of Fire

The apostle Paul further illustrates the believer's responsibility to work with God in the process of living the kind of a Christian life that honors Christ and serves mankind. He supplements the figure of the tilled field with that of constructing a building. As the believer is God's tilled field, tended by Him, so he is likewise "God's building," constructed by Him in cooperation with the believer (1 Co 3:9). The all-important fact to remember, however, is that the foundation for building the Christian life is Christ. His Person and finished redemptive work form the basis for all Christian service. Apart from an experience of His salvation, there can be no works acceptable to God. Paul laid that foundation. Every believer is to build on it (1 Co 3:10-12).

In building a Christian life on the one foundation, Christ, the believer may use various kinds of material — "gold, silver, precious stones [noncombustible material], wood, hay, stubble [combustible]" (1 Co 3:12). The judgment seat of Christ is compared to a fire that will thoroughly test the type of material employed in building. Each believer's work will be tried by fire evidencing its quality before God.

The quality of the believer's life is indicated by the materials used in constructing the building. Gold, in Scripture symbolizes deity;† silver, redemption;‡ precious stones, the beauties of the Redeemer manifested in the redeemed.§ These substances suggest that the believer's works are rendered in true recognition of Christ's deity and Lordship and performed out of genuine love to Christ for His redemptive work, resulting in Christ's glory becoming visible in the believer's ministry. In withstanding fire, they meet with approval at the hand of Him whose eyes are "like a flame of fire" (Rev 1:14). Wood, hay, and straw on the other hand, suggest materials not only combustible, but in an increasing degree. The stubble, or straw, is more inflammable than hay, and the hay more than wood. Also suggested is the fact that these substances decrease sharply in value as building material — wood being much more valuable than either hay or stubble. The figure suggests that the believer's works are performed in the flesh, for self-interest, with scant appreciation of Christ's redemption or with little or no genuine love for Him or sense of obeying His will.

Fire, in Scripture, symbolizes God's holiness (Lev 1:8; Heb 12:29). As such it frequently portrays His judgment upon that which His holiness utterly condemns (Gen 19:24; Mk 9:43-48; Rev 20:15) or disapprovingly rejects, as in the case of the "worthless" works of the carnal Christian (1 Co 3:15; 2 Co 5:10).

Fire also prefigures God's holiness in the manifestation of Himself in that which He approves (Ex 3:2; 13:21; 1 Pe 1:7). This is illustrated in the case of the "good" works of the believer (2 Co

---

† Gold, symbolizing deity in manifestation in Christ, appears prominently in the tabernacle (Ex 25:3), the ark of the covenant (Ex 25:11), the table of shewbread (Ex 25:28-29), the lampstand (Ex 25:31), the tabernacle boards (Ex 25:29), the altar of incense (Ex 30:3), etc.

‡ A half shekel of silver was collected from every Israelite as "atonement money" (Ex 30:16). The silver paid as atonement money was only a token payment looking forward to Christ's redemption and the real price to be paid by Christ's blood (1 Pe 1:18-19).

§The precious stones on the high priest's ephod, carried on his shoulders, and the twelve precious stones on his breastplate signified God's people in the beauties of holiness as supported by Christ and the objects of His intercession (Ex 28:6-29).

5:10). These are not burned up in the fire test at the judgment seat of Christ. Such deeds, tried and found genuine by the omniscient Judge, receive "a reward" (1 Co 3:14).

SAVED AS THROUGH FIRE

The apostle Paul is careful to emphasize that all who appear at the judgment seat of Christ are already saved. In no sense is this judgment penal. Hence the apostle points out very emphatically, "If any man's work is burned up, he shall suffer loss; but he himself shall be saved, yet so as through fire" (1 Co 3:15, NASB).

Imagine yourself waking out of sleep to find your house ablaze. You have no time to save a thing. You flee with only the night clothes on your back. Even these are singed away by the flames that engulf you. You escape with literally nothing but your life.

In this fashion, believers who have lived carnally and carelessly or who have worked for self and self-interest instead of for the Lord will find that all their works have been burned up. They shall have no reward. No trophies to lay at Jesus' feet! No crowns to rejoice in in that day of judgment!

As I stressed in my discussion of the judgment seat of Christ in an earlier volume on prophecy, "Under grace the indispensable distinction must ever be held in mind between salvation and rewards. God offers to the *lost* the free gift of salvation. To the *saved*, He offers rewards for faithful service."[3]

A WARNING TO THE SINNING SAINT

Two perils face the believer at this point. One is to doubt the efficacy and eternity of his salvation when he falls into sin. The other is to hold fast to his unforfeitable salvation, but at the same time to presume upon divine grace and to go on living in sin, imagining that God will not severely discipline him for serious transgression.

The apostle steers the believer safely through these two dangers. He shows that no believer can ever lose his salvation at the judgment seat of Christ, but only his reward. He may pass through the fire of judgment with everything burned up, yet he himself will be saved.

On the other hand, the believer who realizes that his salvation is eternal and unlosable, must also keep in mind that as a redeemed soul, his body is "a temple of God" and "that the Spirit of God dwells" in him (1 Co 3:16, NASB). He is therefore held accountable to keep this sanctuary holy. Here the Spirit of God resides, as the Shekinah glory abode in the holiest place in the Old Testament tabernacle. By keeping himself from sin, the believer is to "glorify God" in his body (1 Co 6:19-20).

Solemnly Paul warns: "If any man destroys the temple of God, God will destroy him, for the temple of God is holy, and that is what you are" (1 Co 3:17, NASB). The word *destroy* (phtheirō, Greek) means to corrupt and as a result, punish with (physical) death.[4]

If a carnal believer scandalously desecrates this holy precinct (cf. 1 Co 5:1-5), God will destroy him by *physical death* (cf. 1 Co 5:5; 11:30-31; 1 Jn 5:16). This is the ultimate in the Father's chastisement of His wayward children. The purpose of physical death is to preclude eternal death.

The latter can never be visited upon a saint because God has given him the gift of eternal life. Eternal life abrogates eternal death. This is why the apostle says that some of the sinning believers at Corinth had been called home to the Lord by the sleep of death. The purpose was that they "might not be condemned along with the world" (1 Co 1:30-32).

Running and Fighting to Win

To illustrate the rewards of the Christian life to be dispensed at the bema seat of Christ, Paul draws a lively figure from the most thrilling spectacle of Greek life — the Isthmian games, celebrated every two years at Corinth (1 Co 9:24-27).

Like the Olympic and Nemaean games, five exercises were included. Of these Paul selects two — footracing and boxing. The first exemplifies the necessity of sustained effort and exertion to win the prize. "All run," but only one wins an award, and that because of superior effort. "Run in such a way that you may win" (NASB).

The second contest (boxing) illustrates the necessity of rigid self-control. "I box in such a way, as not beating the air; but I buffet my body and make it my slave" (1 Co 9:25-26, NASB).

The apostle's self-control is seen in the fact that as a prize-fighter, directing well-aimed blows at his own body, he kept it in subjection. He guarded it against carnal desires. He knew they would sap his spiritual strength and bring him defeat. At the end of the race and at the conclusion of the boxing contest, he was determined he would "stand the test."

Paul realized that in the Greek games all the contestants rigidly disciplined themselves to receive a mere "perishable wreath." This fading prize — a wreath of wild olive or a spray of parsley — contrasts with the "imperishable" awards at Christ's judgment seat. But such rewards could be forfeited by carelessness and carnality. Therefore, the apostle was concerned lest possibly, after he had preached to others, he himself "should be disqualified" (1 Co 9:27, NASB).

Never for a moment did Paul have a qualm concerning his being disapproved in the realm of salvation. However, he did fear, as he does here, being "rejected" in the realm of service and reward.

SAINTS WILL BE GIVEN ASSIGNMENTS

At the judgment seat of Christ, saints will not only be vindicated and rewarded, they will be assigned positions of honor and responsibility in the millennial kingdom and the eternal order following. These appointments will include executive, judicial, and administrative functions. The saints are to sit with Christ in various capacities — ruling, judging, and overseeing.

Overcomers are promised various rewards. Those in the Thyatira period of Romish corruption will be rewarded with the gift of "authority over the [millennial] nations," to rule them with a rod of iron (Ps 2:9; Rev 2:26-27). The blessed and holy who participate in the first resurrection are said to be "priests of God and of Christ" and to "reign with Him for a thousand years" (Rev 20:6, NASB).

Our Lord promised His own disciples rewards in judicial capacity for having left all to follow Him in service. He declared to them: "In the regeneration [the millennial kingdom] when the Son of man shall sit in the throne of his glory, ye also shall sit upon twelve thrones, judging the twelve tribes of Israel" (Mt 19:28).

CROWNS TO LAY AT HIS FEET

Scripture mentions five different crowns that symbolize and summarize the various spheres of achievement and award in the Christian life. The word for crown *(stephanos)* connotes a woven chaplet "put around" *(stephoo)* the head. It denotes the victor's and not the king's crown *(diadēma)*.[5] It has clear reference to the wreath or garland of green awarded as a prize to the winners in the public athletic contests.

"The crown of life" (Ja 1:12) is the martyr's crown. It is distinguished by love for the Lord which proves itself in willingness to suffer for His name, even to the point of death. "Be faithful until death, and I will give you the crown of life" (Rev 2:10, NASB).

"The crown of glory" is the pastor's or elder's crown, awarded by the chief Pastor, when He shall appear. "And when the Chief Shepherd appears, you will receive the unfading crown of glory" (1 Pe 5:4, NASB). This award is made on the basis of faithfully, willingly, and sacrificially ministering the Word to God's flock, in all humility and godliness of example. The reward will be glory in the coming splendor of Christ's earthly and subsequent eternal reign.

"The crown of rejoicing" is the soul-winner's award. "For who is our hope or joy or crown of exultation? Is it not even you, in the presence of our Lord Jesus at His coming? For you are our glory and joy" (1 Th 2:19-20). Paul calls his converts at Philippi, "my joy and crown" (Phil 4:1).

"The crown incorruptible" is the victor's award for those who win in the race of temperance and self-control. They walk by the Spirit and do not fulfill the keen desires of the flesh (1 Co 9:25).

"The crown of righteousness" is the award for those who love Christ's appearing (2 Ti 4:8). They hold and cherish "the blessed hope" (Titus 2:13), undimmed and undiminished throughout their Christian life. They own and recognize that their "citizenship is in heaven, from which also [they] eagerly wait for a Savior, the Lord

Jesus Christ" (Phil 3:20, NASB) and set their affections on the heavenly realm (Col 3:1-4).

THE MARRIAGE OF THE LAMB

The marriage of the Lamb follows the judgment seat of Christ, which is a necessary prelude to it. Once the saints have been judged, rewarded, and assigned places of responsibility and administration in the kingdom, Christ will be in a position to identify Himself publicly with His glorified people. This is set forth under the figure of marriage. Our Lord is pictured as united in marriage to His people. The scene presented in the Revelation is brief but glorious, calling forth intense rejoicing.

"Let us be glad and rejoice, and give honour to him: for the marriage of the Lamb is come, and His wife hath made herself ready" (Rev 19:7).

The call is to honor the Lamb, for this event is not said to be the marriage of the bride but "of the Lamb." All honor is due Him as Creator-Redeemer, God incarnate, the Lamb of God who was slain to take away the sin of the world (Jn 1:29; 1 Pe 1:19; Rev 5:6, 8).

The bride, representing the New Testament church (Jn 14:3; Eph 5:32, 1 Th 4:13-17) is anticipatively introduced as "wife," because she, as the glorified church, is about to be joined to her Head in royal administration and dignity in the kingdom.

The figure of marriage symbolizes the outward, public consummation of the inner spiritual union that now exists between Christ and His church (Ro 6:3-4; 1 Co 12:13; Eph 5:25-27). When the bride becomes the wife, the saints will have entered into the appropriation and enjoyment of all the rewards and assignments dispensed at the judgment seat of Christ. At last they will have realized their eternally predestined association with Him in whom they were chosen "before the foundation of the world" (Eph 1:4).

How wonderful it will be for us to be so gloriously and publicly identified with Him and in this sublime association begin to explore all that God has prepared for those who love Him (1 Co 2:9).

The Glorified Church Ready to Rule

The exultant announcement of the marriage of the Lamb is appended by the declaration that the Lamb's "wife" has made herself ready. The wife (as yet she is actually still the bride) is most interestingly said to make herself ready, as brides are accustomed to do. This action presupposes her being made fit by God through Christ and having her works tested at the bema seat of Christ.

"And to her was granted that she should be arrayed in fine linen, clean and white" (Rev 19:8). The bride's robes symbolize the righteousness of Christ (Ro 3:21-22), bestowed upon her graciously by imputation and sovereignly on the ground of Christ's working in her through the Spirit.

What the crucified and risen Lord merely "began to do and teach" (Ac 1:1), He has continued throughout the age through His body and bride, the church. Therefore, "the righteousnesses" or "righteous acts" (NASB) are those of Christ performed in and through the bride, His wife.

Wedding Guests Invited

Guests are called to the wedding to share this blissful event. "Blessed [happy] are those who are invited to the marriage supper of the Lamb" (Rev 19:9, NASB). These guests are clearly differentiated from the bride, the Lamb's wife; and are evidently Old Testament saints and tribulation martyrs (Jn 3:29; cf. Dan 12:2; Rev 11:18). Whether they share in the bema judgment or are judged separately is not clearly revealed. They do, however, attend the marriage supper.

The "marriage supper" is a part of the marriage of the Lamb. It is a blessed reward for God's own in contrast to the terrible supper of judgment that takes place on earth (Rev 19:17).

6

Rome Revives

THE PREDICTION of the latter-day revival of the ancient Roman empire is one of the most astonishing and incredible aspects of Bible prophecy. Like the prediction of the rapture of the church, the fulfillment of such a development, up until comparatively recent times, has seemed so utterly remote, if not impossible, that the idea has been resisted with much skepticism and even open ridicule.

Yet those who have studied Bible prophecy with any serious intent have always clearly discerned the revival of the ancient Roman empire in the latter years of this age, prior to the second advent of Christ.

WHY EXPECT ROME TO BE REVIVED?

We expect Rome to be revived because prophecies dealing with the latter part of the Roman empire have not as yet been fulfilled (Dan. 2:41-45; 7:8-27). They await fulfillment. This fact is suggested by the specific and detailed fulfillment of the predictions made concerning the former part of the empire as it existed in antiquity (Dan 2:40; 7:7).

Added to this evidence is the minute fulfillment of the predictions made concerning Babylon, Medo-Persia, and Greece, the world empires that preceded Rome, in the prophetic unfolding of the times of the Gentiles (Dan 2:31-45; 7:4-27; 8:20-21).

Since the prophecies concerning the earlier part of the times of the Gentiles have been so minutely fulfilled and verified by hisory (cf. Dan 11:1-35), it is logical for those who honor Scripture as the Word of God to conclude that the predictions concerning the latter part of the same era likewise will be fulfilled to the letter. This is especially true since these prophecies are inseparably connected both by context and by the scope of the visions in which they are set forth.

Geography of Rome Revived

At its greatest extent (A.D. 117), the ancient Roman Empire stretched from the Euphrates River on the east, across Asia Minor and Europe, south of the Danube and east of the Rhine. It included such modern countries as Turkey, Bulgaria, Yugoslavia, Italy, Albania, Austria, Hungary, Switzerland, Spain, Portugal, France, Belgium, the Netherlands, and the southern half of Britain.

The ancient empire also embraced all islands of the Mediterranean Sea and the coastal regions of North Africa now occupied by Morocco, Algeria, Tunisia, and Egypt. At the eastern end of the Mediterranean (the Roman Lake), Syria, Palestine, Transjordan, Iran, and Iraq rounded out the ancient boundaries.

The territory of Rome in its predicted revived form need not be identical with the ancient empire at its greatest extent. However, it will certainly include all of Western Europe outside of Germany and the Soviet Russian bloc, at least in the final stage of its revival.

Strategic Importance of the Middle East

The sphere of ancient Rome, particularly the eastern portion constituting the Middle East, is perhaps the most strategic land on earth. Geographically it is the bridge between three major continents. Besides, it is the gateway to the oceans of the world for southern Europe and western Asia via the Suez Canal.

The Suez Canal is, therefore, one of the world's most strategic waterways. Added to all this, the Middle East is the greatest depository of oil in the world.

By its location, as well as its long history, the Near East is destined to play a crucial role in the future. Should it be considered incredible that Bible prophecy foretells this? Predictions are not lacking, even from non-Christian sources, that the Middle East will once again become the center of world political and economic interest.

LIKELIHOOD OF ROME'S REVIVAL

With the Soviet colossus stalking their borders and threatening to overrun them militarily and economically, does it seem incredible that the countries of western Europe would forget their mutual animosities and get together for self-preservation and protection?

With Russian Communism insidiously exploiting the racial and religious hostilities of the Middle East for its own ends of expansion in this region, the revival of the ancient Roman empire does not appear as unlikely as it might seem to some.

Western Europe will be compelled to get together, as Russia presses harder to dominate the Middle East and make the Mediterranean a Russian Lake instead of a Roman Lake.

Any major confrontation or crisis in the Middle East, or in Europe for that matter, is in Russian hands. None shall come until the Russians decide the moment is ripe. When the nations of western Europe realize the stark reality of this fact, they will be compelled to unite.

Rome's revival is not only plausible, it is inevitable.

WHAT DANIEL SAW

What is now in the process of coming to pass, Daniel foresaw in prophetic vision almost 2600 years ago. By divine help, the young prophet was able to recall and interpret Nebuchadnezzar's strange dream of a huge, resplendent, metallic man (Dan 2:31-35).

The great image, or colossus, as interpreted by Daniel, symbolizes the entire period known in prophecy as "the times of the Gentiles" (Lk 21:24). This is the long period from 605 B.C. till the second advent of Christ. During this era, Jerusalem is chronically, though not continuously, politically subservient to the nations.

Messiah is the smiting stone (Dan 2:34-35). At His second advent, He strikes the image on its feet and destroys the whole Gentile world system catastrophically. Then the stone (Christ) becomes a mountain. This is the millennial rule of Christ (Is 2:2; Rev 13:1; 17:9-11) that fills the whole millennial earth, when the kingdom is restored to Israel (Ac 1:6).

The four metals symbolize the four world empires of "the times of the Gentiles." Babylon is the head of gold, followed by Medo-Persia, the arms and breast of silver. The belly and thighs of bronze portray Greece (under Alexander). Rome is the legs of iron, seen divided into the eastern and western Roman empires.

The western part of the empire fell in A.D. 476. The eastern part survived till 1453.

Revived Rome at the end time appears as ten toes or kingdoms (Dan 2:40-45).

What Daniel Did Not See

Although Daniel saw in the colossus vision "the times of the Gentiles" in panoramic sweep, in the case of the fourth empire, he did not see the interval of many centuries between the decline of Rome and its end-time revival in the ten-kingdom form. This fact is also true of the parallel beast vision (chap. 7).

Ryrie aptly states the case: "It is as if Daniel saw only the mountain peak of the 'leg' form of Rome at and after the first coming of Christ, and then another mountain peak of the 'ten toes' form of Rome, and did not see the years in the valley between."[1]

Such a time gap, as appears here, is not unusual in the prophetic Scriptures. The principle is again aptly illustrated in Daniel's vision of the seventy weeks (490 years) predicted to elapse before Israel is restored to kingdom blessing (Dan 9:20-27; cf. Ac 1:6). The first sixty-nine weeks are consecutive and without a break, being reckoned from the decree to rebuild Jerusalem (445 B.C.).

However, between the sixty-ninth and seventieth week is an extended hiatus. It covers the entire period from Christ's crucifixion and the destruction of Jerusalem in A.D. 70 till the last seven years preceding the second advent of Christ and Israel's restoration to kingdom blessing (Dan 9:26-27).[2]

The prophets often envisioned events such as the first and second comings of Christ in one blended view. Their standpoint was similar to a person who sees two great mountain peaks from a distance. The two may seem to merge into one. Actually a valley hundreds of miles wide may separate them.

NATIONS BRILLIANT BUT BEAST-LIKE

In the colossus vision of Daniel chapter 2, the nations of the period of Gentile supremacy appear as a resplendent, metallic image. The head of dazzling gold, the arms and chest of gleaming silver, the stomach and thighs of bronze, the legs of iron, and the toes of iron and tile symbolize the outward splendor of world governments.

These kingdoms do, indeed, present a fair show. Satan, when he tempted our Lord, showed him all the kingdoms of the world and the glory of them (Mt 4:8).

However, the glory is only an external gloss — a superficial gilt that conceals the true character of the nations. The real nature of the nations is revealed to Daniel to be beast-like rather than manlike (Dan 7:1-28).

Even in their outwardly glorious and manlike aspect, the nations of the satanic world system present a top-heavy image with the much heavier metals at the top tending to topple the colossus.[3] Besides, it has an extremely flimsy foundation of iron, weakened by intermixture with unadhering clay (Dan 2:34-35). All the glory will come crashing down to ruin when it will be struck by Christ, the smiting stone, at His second advent.

BEWARE — A NONDESCRIPT BEAST

Daniel glimpsed the beast-like quality of the nations in chapter 7 of his remarkable prophecy. The head of gold (Babylon) appears as a winged lion. The arms and chest of silver (Medo-Persia) are seen as a voracious bear. The belly and thighs of bronze (Greece) appear as a winged four-headed leopard. The legs of iron (Rome) are symbolized as a dreadful, terrible, nondescript beast, exceedingly strong. It has great iron teeth with which it mercilessly devours its prey, and horrible feet and claws with which it tramples down in death what it does not devour.

This fourth beast is different from all the beasts that preceded it and has "ten horns." These horns portray kings. They correspond to the ten toes of the colossus. These kings arise and comprise the rulers of the revived Roman empire of the end time.

Daniel was especially troubled concerning the terrible fourth beast. The sight of its ferocity and awful cruelty horrified him. The ten horns of the beast, he was shown, will constitute the form in which this fourth or Roman empire will exist when the whole fabric of Gentile world power will be crushed by Christ at His second advent (Dan 2:44-45; 7:9).

The Rome of Nero, Domitian, Trajan, Marcus Aurelius, and Diocletian horribly persecuted and put to death God's people. The same imperial power, resurrected in a form more terrifying and awful, will exceed these atrocities.

Look out for the nondescript beast! The Bible pictures the beast's great iron teeth crushing and devouring God's people. Its dread claws of bronze are seen breaking the saints to pieces, and its monstrous feet crush them as it ruthlessly tramples down everything in its way (Dan 7:19).

Introducing the Antichrist

While Daniel was occupied with the dreadful fourth beast, portraying Rome both in its ancient aspect and in its revived ten-kingdom form of the last days, suddenly he saw a most unusual thing. Before his eyes, as he gazed at the ten horns on the beast's head, there arose another "little horn" (Dan 7:8).

At once this "little horn" commands attention. He is different from the rest — stronger, more sinister, more diabolic and blasphemous. Ruthlessly he crushes three of the ten kings. So completely does he exterminate them that the identity of their kingdom is wiped out. So rapid and astounding are his victories that he is catapulted to the headship of the fourth world empire.

He is Satan's imitation of Christ. He is "the prince that shall come" (Dan 9:26), "the beast out of the sea" (Rev 13:1). He is called the "abomination" (Dan 12:11; Mt 24:15) because he curses God, arrogates deity to himself, and demands worship of all men. He is also styled "the man of lawlessness" (2 Th 2:4) and "the willful king" (Dan 11:36-45) because he utterly disregards the law of God and man to achieve his satanic goal of taking over the earth.

ANTICHRIST VERSUS CHRIST

Satan's false Christ, the Antichrist, is the antithesis of the true Christ of God. As Christ was God incarnate, the Antichrist will be Satan incarnate (Rev 13:2).

As Christ was immeasurably filled with the Holy Spirit, the Antichrist will be immeasurably energized by demonic power (Rev 13:2).

As Christ was absolutely loyal to God's Word and always did God's will, the Antichrist will utterly oppose God's Word and do only his own will.

As the sovereignty of the earth has been given to Christ by virtue of creation and redemption, the Antichrist will seek to overturn God's plan for the earth and seize that sovereignty for himself.

ANTICHRIST — THE ROMAN PRINCE

That the Antichrist is a Roman ruler appears from the fact that, as the "little horn," he came up on the head of the dreadful fourth beast (Rome revived) and conquered three of the ten horns (Dan 7:8, 20, 24-25). In this manner he will make himself supreme head of the empire.

The fact that the Antichrist is a Roman prince is also a clear inference from Daniel's vision of the seventy weeks (Dan 9:26-27).' Messiah, as predicted, was "cut off" in death *after* the sixty-ninth week. During the interval between the sixty-ninth and seventieth week, "the people of the prince that shall come," as predicted, destroyed the city of Jerusalem in A.D. 70. These people were obviously the Romans.

It clearly follows, then, that "the prince that shall come" is also Roman. This is substantiated by the unbroken continuity of the fourth empire, linking the last stage with the first stage, which was obviously Roman.

ANTICHRIST AND THE COVENANT WITH ISRAEL

As head of the revived Roman empire, the Antichrist alone will have power to make the predicted last-day treaty with Israel (Dan 9:27). The alliance will be signed, obviously, only after the "little horn" of Daniel 7 has conquered the ten kings and attained a position of supremacy over them, in this way securing authority to conclude such a treaty.

The regathering of the Jews to Palestine and the emergence of the Israeli nation in the twentieth century, together with the growing likelihood of a federation of European states, place these predicted events in a new light. Once considered impossible and scorned as ridiculous, they now appear not only as possible, but as highly probable, if not eventually inevitable.

COMING UP — THE UNITED STATES OF EUROPE

The Bible always did predict a last-day union of federated states of Europe preceding the second advent of Christ. Serious students of prophecy have readily comprehended this amazing disclosure. They foretold such a development even when the interminable quarrels and divisions of Europe made them a virtual laughingstock to worldly-wise politicians and political prognosticators.

As early as 1914, a committee was formed for the promotion of a European federation. This movement manifested itself after World War I in the short-lived League of Nations.

Not until after World War II, however, did the idea of a united Europe crystallize into anything more substantial than a utopian dream. Even then progress was slow. Two world wars had at least taught men that force is not the best way to settle disputes. As a result, the United Nations came into being, embodying for the first time in history the principle of world government.

Unfortunately, however, World War II created a military and political colossus on the doorstep of Europe. Soon all of western Europe found a superpowerful enemy breathing down its neck and threatening to swallow up its territory and overrun it politically and ideologically.

From 1939-1945 the Soviet Union annexed 181,610 square miles of Europe, comprising a population of over twenty-two million people. Poland, Latvia, Estonia, Lithuania, Romania, Czechoslovakia, and East Germany were among the countries forced into the Soviet Union.

A war-weary world stood aghast at Russian ruthlessness, too exhausted to call the Soviet bluff and risk triggering World War III.

Even the United States of America, the other supergiant emerging from World War II, has been badgered and tormented by Soviet duplicity and ambition in these territorial takeovers and in such unprincipled demonstrations of Soviet treachery as the infamous Berlin blockade.

All the while, pressure has been pressing down relentlessly on western Europe. Its voice is stern and unrelenting: "As long as you remain divided, you are no match for the Soviet Union. You must unite."[5]

You may rely upon it! *Europe will unite!*

PROPHETIC SIGNIFICANCE OF THE EUROPEAN COMMON MARKET

This economic community came into existence as a result of a treaty signed in Rome on March 25, 1957. It consisted of six nations — France, the German Federal Republic, Italy, Belgium, the Netherlands, and Luxembourg. Popularly known as the European Common Market, this organization grew out of the earlier Coal and Steel Community, formed in 1952 by these nations. Their goal was to develop a wider economic alliance that would foster mutual prosperity.[6]

By tariff reductions, permitting the free flow of goods from one country to another, and the unhindered transfer of available labor, the goal has been reached to a large degree. As a result, many forecast an ultimate United States of Europe, as other nations have joined the Common Market or a similar organization of other European nations. Such a group was organized on May 4, 1960 and called the Free Trade Association.

It is doubtful whether the Common Market or the Free Trade Association, as they now exist, have direct prophetic repercussions.

However, these organizations show the practicability of such economic pooling of resources.

Unification on the economic level is not far removed from political union. It is certainly conceivable that under pressure from the Soviet Union, western Europe, in precisely the territory covered by ancient Rome, would see a ten-nation economic-political merger, whose industrial and military might would equal or surpass that of the Soviet Union.

This is what men now predict may happen.[7] This is what the European Common Market demonstrates can happen. This is what the prophetic Word declares *will happen!*

WHEN ROME AGAIN RULES THE WORLD

Rome ruled the ancient world. Revived Rome will rule the world before Christ returns. Two preliminary phases of revived Rome will precede the final world dominant stage.

The first phase will witness the formation of the ten-kingdom federation of western and southern Europe rimming the Mediterranean. This will evidently come into being before the tribulation period.

The second phase will develop with the rise of the Antichrist (Daniel's "little horn") who will root out three kings and make himself the absolute ruler of a consolidated kingdom. This will evidently occur at the beginning of the tribulation period.

The third and final phase embraces Rome as the dominant world power under the Antichrist (Dan 7:23; Rev 13:7-8). This will evidently occur at the beginning of the great tribulation, and continue during the last half of the week, three and one-half years before Christ's glorious advent (Rev 13:35). This fact appears since the Roman beast (the Antichrist) is destroyed by Christ's coming (Rev 19:20; 20:10).

WHAT HAPPENS TO RUSSIA?

How could revived Rome possibly rule the world without clashing with Russia? Certainly such a confrontation would be inescapable if the Soviet were still a world power.

The prophetic Word does not directly explain how Rome comes to rule the world. The plausible explanation is that Russia is utterly destroyed by divine intervention when she challenges the Roman empire by invading Israel, then in league with Rome.

So completely are the Soviet and her satellites exterminated in the battle of Gog and Magog (Eze 38:1 — 39:24), that the Roman ruler has no major political power thwarting his plan to take over the whole earth.

Apparently he declares himself the ruler of the world by public proclamation over world television and radio and proceeds by diabolic ruthlessness to make good his claim.

WHO IS LIKE THE BEAST?

Now the world is ready to follow the Roman ruler, apparently invincible and supported by satanic power. The adoring cry of godless earth dwellers is "Who is like unto the beast? who is able to make war with him?" (Rev 13:4).

But the horrible thing is, wicked men do not merely follow the beast as a political ruler. They worship the dragon (Satan) who gives him his power and they worship the beast himself, since he is the Antichrist and demands worship (Rev 13:4, 8).

The false prophet exercises all the diabolic power of the beast and causes all men, on pain of death, to worship the beast (Rev 13:12). With a full array of diabolic miracles, he deludes men to bow down to the image of the beast (Rev 13:14-15).

All those who worship the beast receive the mark of the beast in their right hand or in their forehead. Only those who receive the mark, and so attest their denial of God and His Christ, will be able to buy or sell (Rev 13:16-18).

No wonder that Daniel foresaw that this fiendish monster would make war with the saints and prevail against them (Dan 11:21)! What stark horror faces anyone who names the name of God and confesses Christ in those gruesome days!

In that dread hour, man's apostasy from God and His Word will have reached its frightful fruition. Only devil-worshipers, who bow to the Antichrist and yield to the delusions of the false prophet, will escape death in the most hellish persecution Satan, "the liar and murderer" (Jn 8:44), has ever invented.

The World Religion of Rome

Little do people today realize this is the dismal road toward which the present-day widespread departure from God's Word is heading. After the true church has been translated to heaven, the false church left behind will develop into a gigantic ecclesiastical organization of tremendous wealth, prestige, and political power. (See chap. 3.)

This false church, symbolized by the gaudy harlot of Revelation 17, will ride into the heyday of her prestige as the protégée of the revived Roman empire (Rev 17:3).

But when the Antichrist takes supreme control of the empire, he, with his confederate kings, turns against the harlot ecclesiastical system and utterly destroys it (Rev 17:16-17).

In its place, the Roman ruler institutes the final world religion. This is Satan's masterpiece, whose diabolic creed is:

Satan must be worshiped instead of God.

Believe in Antichrist instead of Christ.

The false prophet must be followed instead of the Holy Spirit.

The satanic trinity must replace the divine Trinity.

The goal of this world religion: banish the name of God and His Christ from the earth and destroy the Jew in whom God's plans for the earth center.

Take over the earth for Satan and his followers, so that Satan and his false Christ may be worshiped instead of God and His Christ.

No wonder Satan's strategy begins by turning men away from God's Word.

7

The Russian Bear Rampages

THE PHENOMENAL RISE of Russia as a superpower since World War II is one of the significant aspects of the present-day troubled world situation. This great colossus with vaulting ambitions of world conquest has become the principal competitor of the United States of America for world leadership.

Russian power presents the world with a new and dangerous threat to peace and security. Dedicated to atheistic, materialistic Communism, the Soviet Union has not only enslaved the conscience and will of its own 209,000,000 people, it seeks to extend its godless political philosophy and control over the whole earth.

The question that arises is important. Does the remarkable ascendency of such a God-denying nation in our day have prophetic import?

Is RUSSIA IN BIBLE PROPHECY?

It is unthinkable that this vast God-defying power would not be included in the scope of things to come as set forth in the Bible. It would be equally incredible, if scripture prophecy is reliable, not to expect this godless giant at least to be mentioned indirectly. On this point there is scarcely any disagreement among serious students of Bible prophecy.

Most Bible scholars agree that Russia is referred to prophetically in Ezekiel chapters 38 and 39, and under the title of "king of the north" in Daniel 11:40 and in other passages.

However, because the word *Russia* does not actually occur in the English Bible, few would say that this nation is referred to directly by name. Yet there is not lacking evidence that the word *Rosh* in the Hebrew of Ezekiel 38:2-3 and 39:1 is not only a proper name, but almost certainly is to be equated with Russia.

The American Standard Version, following the Hebrew (*Rosh*) and the Septuagint (*Rhos*) correctly renders "Gog," the leader of the northern confederacy, as "the prince of Rosh."

The rendering "chief prince" (KJV and RSV) is based upon the interpretive rendering of the Hebrew "prince of head," that is, "head or chief prince." This translation construes the Hebrew *rosh* as a common noun meaning head, instead of correctly viewing it as a proper name (*Rosh*).

Is Rosh Russia?

Linguistic evidence for the equation is confessedly only presumptive, since Rosh (possibly a Scythian tribe) is yet unidentified. However, when other evidence is considered, there can be little doubt that the reference is to the nation Russia. In fact, in the light of the end-time prophetic picture, there is no other reasonable alternative.

Concerning the linguistic evidence, the words of William Gesenius, the famous nineteenth-century Hebrew lexicographer, are still valid. "Rosh is the proper name of a northern nation . . . probably to be equated with *the Russians*, who are described by the Byzantine writers of the tenth century under the name of the *Ros*, as inhabiting the northern parts of the Taurus. And also [referred to] by Ibn Foszlan, an Arabian writer of the same period, under the name *Rus*, as dwelling on the river Wolga [Volga].[1]

The Russian name for Russia (*Rossiya*) doubtless stems from *Rosh*, with suffix added. The English form, *Russia*, apparently derives from Slavonic *Rus*.[2] Ancient words in evolving to their modern forms frequently undergo a change of vowels, while the consonants tend to remain the same.

WHO IS THE PRINCE OF ROSH?

The prince of Rosh is a northern leader who spearheads a last-day invasion of Israel. He is Russian because he comes from "the uttermost parts of the north" (Eze 38:6, 15; 39:2). Geographically, the *only* nation in the territory to the extreme north of Palestine, in fact extending to the Arctic Circle, is Russia. This adds further evidence that Rosh is Russia.

This great leader heads the northern power bloc of Gog and Magog, second only to the western confederation of nations comprising the revived Roman empire. The ethnic evidence, in addition to the geographic, also indicates that this leader is Russian.

"The prince of Rosh" is also "prince of Meshech and Tubal." The names associated with the northern leader are identified as sons of Japheth (Gen 10:2). The descendants of Japheth, after the deluge, migrated from Asia Minor to the north beyond the Black Sea and the Caspian Sea, territory now in the Soviet Union.

Meshech and Tubal are the Mushki and the Tabali of the Assyrian records. Notices of them in the Assyrian period (1100-612 B.C.) place their home in Asia Minor. But by Herodotus' time (ca. 450 B.C.), they had removed farther north to the region of the Black Sea in southern Russia.[3] In subsequent centuries, they pressed farther north into the Volga River basin in the general region of Moscow.

GOG OF THE LAND OF MAGOG

Gog is evidently an ideal and well-known title adopted by Ezekiel from the famous king of Lydia, Gugu or Gyges (ca. 680-648 B.C.). The name aptly portrays the exercise of ruthless, godless power. In Greek legend, Gyges was mythologized into a hundred-handed giant, who made war on the gods, but was slain by Hercules and eternally punished in Tartarus.[4]

Ezekiel, like other Old Testament prophets, couched his prophecies in terms of the personalities, events, and local color of his own time. During his prophetic ministry, a horde of northern Asiatics, termed "Scythians" by the Greeks, and likely embracing the Mushki and the Tabali of the Black Sea area, undertook an expedition against Egypt.[5]

The term *Magog,* denoting the country of Gog, is apparently also an ideal designation employed by the prophet. It specifies the territory over which Gog extends his dominion. Magog is mentioned as a progenitor of Japhetic peoples in Gen 10:2, along with Meshech and Tubal.

GOG AGAINST GOD

Gog's hatred of God is manifested in his hatred of God's people. The ruthless communist leader is pictured as a rampaging beast, ready to trample down God's people, the Jews, to seize Palestine to realize his long-desired dream of controlling the Near East and eventually the world.

But in this dark hour, God's power and sovereignty shine forth. God declares to the rampaging Russian bear: "I will turn thee about, and put hooks in thy jaws, and I will bring thee forth" (Eze 38:4, ASV). God demonstrates He is above Gog. The wild beast shall be chained to do only what God will allow him to do and only that which Gog's folly makes necessary to be done.

Gog's folly is the blasphemy of atheistic, materialistic Communism. This evil system will come to its final terrible fruition in him. He, as its last and most powerful representative, finds its crimes concentrated in himself and his doom.

Gog's defeat, with the destruction of his vast military machine, represents the divine avenging the colossal insult atheistic Communism has heaped upon God's holy name and cause. It also portrays God's avenging the blood of millions of His people slaughtered during the Bolshevik Revolution and under Stalin and Khrushchev. It highlights the damage and the hurt inflicted on other millions — the lies, the blasphemies, the violence, and the God-hating and God-defying efforts of communist leaders to destroy every vestige of God and Christianity.

GOD AGAINST GOG

Gog has been violently and implacably opposed to God. God

in turn is graphically envisioned as climactically opposed to Gog. Twice the Lord declares His unalterable opposition. "Behold, I am against thee, O Gog, prince of Rosh, Meschech, and Tubal" (Eze 38:3; 39:1, ASV).

The high-sounding titles of the communist giant are repeated to emphasize his proud self-confidence and haughty contempt of God and God's people.

Soviet duplicity and ambition will have come to full fruition, when the Russian high command issues the order to invade Israel. The enormous wealth of the Dead Sea, the prosperity of the Israeli state, and access to the oil of the Near East are only part of the rich prize the Russians determine to seize.

The godless political philosophy of the Russian Communists will blind them to the fact that in attacking God's people Israel they are fighting against God. Their blatant atheism and trust in the god of material and military power, instead of the God of heaven, will delude them into their supreme folly of attempting to trample down Israel to attain their long-desired goals.

"And it shall come to pass in that day, when Gog shall come against the land of Israel, saith the Lord Jehovah, that my wrath shall come up into my nostrils" (Eze 38:18, ASV).

Gog has been against God. Now God is against Gog! All the anger of His outraged holiness, so long pent-up against a wicked system that has blasphemed His name and harassed and murdered His people, is now let loose in the full fury of judgment.

Gog's Allies

A number of nations are associated with Russia in the invasion of Israel and the plan to take over the Near East: Persia, Cush, Put, Gomer, and Togarmah.

Persia is present-day Iran, south of Russia. It stretches southward from the southern end of the Caspian Sea to the Persian Gulf. Eastward it extends from the Tigris River to the borders of India on the southeast, Afghanistan on the east, and Russia on the northeast.

Cush is evidently present-day Iraq, west of Iran, southeast of modern Turkey, north of Saudi Arabia, and east of Syria and Trans-jordan. Cush is presented originally in connection with Babylonia. (Later, Cush's descendants migrated to Ethiopia.) Today, Iraq occupies the middle and lower Tigris-Euphrates valley (Gen 2:13; 10:8-12). Cush is likely to be identified with the ancient kingdom of Kish in lower Babylonia from which the emperors of the third millennium B.C. took their titles as kings of the world.[6]

With Iran and Iraq then in the Soviet bloc, Russia will have access to the vast oil reserves of these two nations. This circumstance will apparently enable her great war machine to roll into Israel in an attempt to take over the entire Near East.

Put is apparently modern Libya, an Arab state west of Egypt, in North Africa, as is known from ancient Persian inscriptions. However, a country located in present-day Syria or western Turkey would rather be expected.

Gomer represents the Cimmerians of classical antiquity. They came from Asia beyond the Caucasus Mountains and invaded the regions of Asia Minor in the seventh century B.C. Their territory now comprises southern Russia.

Togarmah is Tegarama in Armenia, southwest of the Black Sea, now a part of southern Russia (Armenian Soviet Socialist Republic).

PROPHETIC STAGE BEING SET

Two great events of comparatively recent times are setting the stage for the fulfillment of the remarkable predictions of Ezekiel chapters 38 and 39. Both of these events have occurred since World War II. One is the phenomenal rise of Russia, not only as a world power, but as a godless nation that hates the Jew and is determined to conquer the world.

The other is the creation of the nation Israel in 1948 with the repatriation of hundreds of thousands of Jews and the restoration of the land to prosperity and promise.

Both of these significant developments, which before the twentieth century seemed so very remote, if not impossible, were foreseen and foretold by the prophet Ezekiel almost 2600 years ago.

RUSSIA IN THE END TIME

Ezekiel envisions Russia at the end of the age as a superpower. Although Russia was an important nation before World War II, it did not become the mighty giant it is today until after World War II. The magnitude of the strength of the Soviet military force that is predicted to invade Palestine is emphasized by the huge quantities of war material involved and the astronomical number of the casualties.

Seven months will be required to bury the dead. It will take seven years to burn the debris resulting from the defeat (Eze 39:1-20).

Until the present generation, Russia was not in a position to fulfill the details of Ezekiel's prophecy. But today she is! She has the material resources. She has the military strength. She has the scientific know-how. She has the godless political philosophy. She has hatred for Israel. She has vaulting ambitions in the Middle East, the Mediterranean area, the Suez Canal, and the Indian Ocean.

And Israel, tiny as she is, but strategically important, is the one barrier that stands in the way of Russian control of the Middle East and her dream of eventual world domination.

ISRAEL IN THE END TIME

The amazing thing about Ezekiel's vision of Russia at the end of the age is its inseparable connection with the rebirth of the nation Israel. When the Soviet invades Israel, the Jewish people will be regathered from their worldwide dispersion of many centuries. They will be restored as a peaceful and prosperous nation in Palestine. Amazingly, the prophet saw the people dwelling securely in unwalled cities without bars and gates (Eze 38:11).

This detail of the prediction is of immense importance. It dates the vision as still future. Unwalled towns were practically unknown in antiquity. Any city of importance was surrounded by a wall with gates and bars for protection against enemies. But in our times, because of modern weapons of warfare, such precautions are useless.

Israel today is a land of fabulous new cities and not one has a wall. Jerusalem's wall is a relic of the past, not a modern necessity. How did the ancient prophet know that at the end of the age, cities would be unwalled? The answer, of course, is simple. He was guided by the Spirit of inspiration to pen the sure word of prophecy. His own wisdom had nothing to do with the matter.

Russia's Invasion and Israel's Rebirth

Ezekiel's prophecy, it is evident, could not have been fulfilled prior to World War II. Just as Russia did not become a supergiant to fulfill her end-time role till after World War II, so Israelites did not return to Palestine in large numbers till after 1945, to become a nation in 1948. Before that time, Russia was in no position to invade Palestine, and if she had, there would have been no Jewish nation to invade.

Since the realization of national status, the number of Israelites in Palestine has doubled. The miracle of Israel's amazing rise as an important and prosperous nation has astounded the world and will arouse evil designs in the scheming Russians.

Who but a believer in Bible prophecy would ever have envisioned Israel today? A nation in its own land, under its own flag, speaking its own language (Hebrew), and zealously restoring its ancient home to a country of fertility and wealth!

"To Take a Spoil and to Take a Prey"

The prophetic Word is quite explicit as to why Russia will invade Palestine at the end of the age. Israel will have become very wealthy (Eze 38:12-13). Russia will covet and attempt to seize that wealth.

Up until comparatively recent times, this prediction seemed to be pure nonsense, even to some evangelical students of prophecy.

Before the birth of the Israeli state, Palestine was anything but a prize and a prey. Barren, desolate, treeless, eroded, bestrewn with stones, it was mainly the homeland of impoverished, backward Arabs, who were for the most part Bedouins. It had no wealth. Where the land was not eroded and agriculturally worthless, malarial swamps infested with mosquitoes made civilized life impossible. But Israel has effected a miracle. Swamps have been drained and converted to the finest farmland. Eroded slopes have been planted with trees. Stony fields have been cleared and cultivated. Dry areas have been irrigated. The land is once again "flowing with milk and honey" as in Bible times. Agricultural wealth is coming to Israel.

Another source of wealth is the incalculably valuable minerals deposited in the Dead Sea. Very much alive today, this magic miser for centuries has been receiving its wealth from the waters of the Jordan and hoarding it, like some mystical Fort Knox, to help finance Israel's God-ordained role "in the latter years" of this age (Eze 38:8).

Beside this, the richest oil reserves in the world lie to the east of Israel in the Middle East. Russia realizes that the nation that will control those oil lands must control Israel. Israel in turn is the door to the Suez Canal, to Africa, the Indian Ocean and the world. Prize enough under any consideration!

Russia's Invasion of Israel and the USA's Role

With the United States and the Soviet Union the two great superpowers of the world today, the question may well be asked, What position, if any, will the United States take in Russia's invasion of Israel?

To some it may appear presumptuous even to imagine that the prophetic Word would throw any light on this question. Yet in consideration of the wonders of the prophetic Scriptures in general, one might expect to find at least some reliable guidelines. Personally, I believe there is such information, particularly since the stage is being set for these events, and their fulfillment does not appear to be far distant.

This does not mean that the United States is mentioned by name in Scripture. She most certainly is not. Nor does it mean that there is any direct or specific reference to the United States in the Bible. It does mean, however, that there are indirect references that are broad enough to include the United States. Interestingly enough, such a reference occurs in this very prophecy of Russia's invasion of Israel in Ezekiel chapters 38 and 39.

When Russia begins the invasion of Palestine, certain maritime and commercial nations are represented as lodging what is apparently a protest. "Sheba, and Dedan, and the merchants of Tarshish, with all the young lions thereof, shall say unto thee, Art thou come to take the spoil? hast thou assembled thy company to take the prey? . . . to take great spoil?" (Eze 38:13, ASV).

Sheba and Dedan were peoples of Arabia, east of Palestine, who traded by land. The merchants of Tarshish were traders by sea and represent maritime peoples and nations west of Palestine.

Tarshish was a land on the western Mediterranean Sea coast (probably Spain), rich in copper and other minerals (Jer 10:9; Eze 27:12; Jonah 1:3; 4:2). There copper was smelted and transported in "ships of Tarshish" in exchange for produce from the eastern Mediterranean.* The term *Tarshish* in time came to denote any land bordering the sea where mining, smelting, and trading in metal ore were carried on.[7]

Hence, Ezekiel's reference to "Tarshish and its young lions" apparently is a broad enough expression to include *all* the younger nations, not only of the Old World but the New. This evidently includes the United States of America, since it was founded by Old World nations. The equivalent in today's terminology would be "the West" or NATO nations in general, in distinction to the Eastern or Soviet bloc.

In the present arms race between the United States and the Soviet Union, the latter will apparently win out. When Russia feels ready to strike Palestine, the United States apparently will have receded to a secondary position, at least militarily. All America will do, or be able to do, is to lodge an innocuous protest (Eze 38:13). To this, the powerful Soviet supergiant will, of course, pay scant attention.

---

* *Tarshish* stems from an old Semitic root found in Akkadian, meaning to melt, be melted. It denotes any place where mining and smelting were carried on. See Albright, "New Light on the Early History of Phoenician Colonization," *Bulletin of the American Schools of Oriental Research*, 83 (1941): 14ff.

WHEN THE SOVIET ORDERS ATTACK

When will Gog order his tremendous war machine to strike defenseless Israel to seize a ripe plum? Some contend he will do so before the rapture. Others say after the rapture at the beginning of the tribulation or at the end of it. Others place it at the beginning of the kingdom or even at the end of it.

The context of the event in the prophecy of Ezekiel clearly indicates a time when Israel is regathered to Palestine as a nation (chap. 37) and is enjoying a period of rest and security (chaps. 38-39) *before* kingdom blessing (chaps. 40-48).

Although Israel will be enjoying such a time of security and quiet during the kingdom age, it cannot occur then, because war will be outlawed during that period (Is 2:4). Besides, the godless will be judged and excluded from the kingdom (Mt 25:31-46). It would be impossible for such a lawless nation as Russia to exist then.

Nor can it occur when Satan is loosed at the end of the kingdom age (Rev 20:7-9). Obviously, Israel will not be at rest then. Besides, this is utterly at variance with the context in the book of Ezekiel.

Moreover, the invasion cannot occur now. Today Israel is an armed camp, surrounded by deadly foes who entertain one consuming passion: to crush her. Nor can the event transpire during the great tribulation as a phase of Armageddon. Not only will Israel not be secure, she will then be in the maelstrom of her greatest woe.

The evident moment when Russia will strike is the first half of Daniel's seventieth week (Dan 9:27). Israel at that time will be under a seven-year treaty of protection and peace with the head of the revived Roman empire in the West.

The Soviet will realize the time has finally come. It is now or never. Suddenly the Soviet high command gives the order. Like a whirlwind, the great Russian military machine, poised on the borders of the Near East, sweeps down upon the Holy Land, as Ezekiel saw in prophetic vision over two and a half milleniums ago.

DANIEL'S VISION OF RUSSIA'S ATTACK ON ISRAEL

The full, prophetic revelation concerning Russia's role in the end-time events that climax in Armageddon has frequently been lost sight of by students of prophecy. The reason for this is the common failure to comprehend Daniel's extended disclosure on this subject (Dan 11:35-45) and to realize this pivotal passage most significantly supplements Ezekiel's prophecy contained in chapters 38 and 39. Practically all prophetic scholars agree that Daniel 11:36-40 refers to the Antichrist, the head of the revived Roman empire, acting through his puppet ally, the Israeli leader in Jerusalem. Few, however, seem to discern that "the king of the north" (Russia), introduced in the latter part of verse 40, *not* the Antichrist, remains the subject of the rest of the chapter.

To assume the subject reverts back to the Antichrist or Roman ruler is at variance with the grammar of the passage. Once "the king of the north" is introduced, there is nothing to indicate that he does not continue to be the subject of the remaining verses. To insist that the Antichrist is reintroduced is based upon assumption, not the plain, grammatical meaning of these verses.

Moreover, the continuity of the thought of this section argues for the same conclusion. The invasion launched by the king of the north against Palestine is the subject introduced and developed in the succeeding context.[8] The perpetrator of this attack from the north is not the Antichrist; Russia and her satellites are responsible.

Failure of many prophetic students to apprehend the real subject of this passage has occasioned a great deal of obscurity and confusion in fixing Russia's role in the chronology of end-time events. Consequently, Ezekiel's great prophecy of the Soviet's latter-day assault on Israel (chaps. 38-39) is frequently left dangling in the air with no definite clue where to place it in relation to the events of Armageddon.

The context, as supplied by Daniel's vision, however, dovetails with Ezekiel's foreview and also suggests that the time is the first part of Daniel's seventieth week when Israel has entered a treaty with the Antichrist.

RUSSIA DOUBLE-CROSSES THE ARABS

That the Soviets will eventually betray the Arab world is revealed by Daniel. This great prophet of the times of the Gentiles predicts that the end-time holocaust will be set off by the king of the south (Egypt and the Pan-Arab bloc) attacking the Israeli leader in league with the Antichrist, the head of the United States of Europe. "And at the time of the end shall the king of the south contend with him [the Israeli leader]" (Dan 11:40, ASV).

This attack on Israel by the Arabs in league with Russia will furnish the grand opportunity for the Soviets to unleash their mighty war machine in a blitzkrieg invasion of the Middle East, by both land and sea. Daniel also saw this pivotal event. "And the king of the north shall come against him [the Israeli leader] like a whirlwind, with chariots, and with horsemen, and with many ships; and he shall enter in the countries [of the Near East] and shall overthrow and pass through" (Dan 11:40).

For many centuries, Russia has dreamed of dominating the Near East. To secure the land bridge of Palestine and Egypt, yielding year-round harbors and ready access to the oceans of the world, it will be necessary for Russia to destroy not only her inveterate foes, the Israelis, but her alleged friends, the Arabs, as well. When the time comes, and the decision must be made, Russia will not hesitate a moment to attempt to do both.

Daniel definitely declares the invading Russian power "shall enter also into the glorious land [Palestine]," and sweep down into Egypt, seizing its wealth and securing the land bridge of access to the Suez Canal and the Indian Ocean (Dan 11:41-43).

It is at this point the Russian leader hears disturbing news that the armies of the Antichrist north of Egypt and the Oriental armies on the east are mobilizing to challenge him. As a result, he hurries back to destroy the Israelis. There in Palestine, as his armies are about to annihilate the nation Israel, "He shall come to his end, and none shall help him" (Dan 11:45).

Gog Meets His Waterloo

The prophet Ezekiel envisions in detail the utter destruction of the enemy. Singularly enough, the overpowering invading force evidently is not crushed by an opposing army or armaments of any kind. God intervenes! Gog is brought to ruin by the hand of God! (Eze 38:18-23).

Then God will fight for His people Israel as He fought for them in ancient times. He turns the enemy upon himself so that Gog's hordes slay each other, as did the Amalekites in the days of Gideon (Judg 7:22). He sends pestilence upon them, as He did upon Sennacherib's hosts (2 Ki 19:35).

He beats them down with drenching rains and crushes them with huge hailstones, as He did for Joshua and the Israelites at Gibeon (Jos 10:10-11). He detonates their explosives with lightning blasts and annihilates them with brimstone.

Gog has grossly insulted God. Hence, God must be magnified among those by whom He has been belittled. He must be sanctified among those by whom His holy name has been blasphemed (Eze 38:21-23). Godless, atheistic Communists have brazenly affronted God's deity and glory. They must be crushed by God Himself.

No man nor instrument of man must receive the glory of Gog's defeat. God alone will be exalted in the overthrow of that which has so grossly dishonored Him and brought such terrible woe upon His people.

What's Ahead for Russia?

With the Soviet Union relentlessly pressing ahead in the present-day arms race, the question may well be asked, Will Russia ever realize its dream of world domination? While Scripture gives no clue as to what Russia might do between now and the invasion of Israel, one thing is clear. There is no room in God's prophetic program for a Soviet-dominated world empire.

Scripture outlines only four world empires. Russia is *not* one of them. The final world empire will be Roman, not Russian. This will be succeeded by Christ's earthly kingdom.

Bible prophecy reveals that Russia, instead of becoming a world-dominating empire, is headed for colossal defeat. This will be a judgment from God because of the blasphemy and godlessness of the atheistic, materialistic, political philosophy upon which it has extended its power.

RUSSIA AND THE REVIVED ROMAN EMPIRE

The annihilation of Soviet military might, occasioned by the invasion of Israel, will obviously destroy the balance of power in the world situation in the first half of the tribulation. The Roman empire comprising the Western confederacy of nations, coming under the control of the Roman prince (the Antichrist), will suddenly be catapulted into a position to dominate the whole world (Rev 13:4).

COMMUNISM AND WORLD RELIGION

Scripture prophecy definitely indicates that Russia as a political power will go down. However, Communism as an atheistic religion, which has already swept within its folds half the world's population, will be the forerunner of the future world religion that will sweep the earth under the Antichrist, the head of the revived Roman empire.

Denying that God exists, and recognizing only material force, the religious aspect of Communism will enable the Antichrist to destroy all religion or any god previously worshiped. In its place he will set himself up as the sole object of universal worship and compel men to bow down to him.

This is the world religion that will hold sway after the harlot system has been destroyed (Rev 17) and Antichrist reigns supreme. This ultimate false religion, of course, will not be the political-religious system we know today. But present-day Communism, under which untold millions are being schooled in atheism and materialism, will certainly be the forerunner and prepare the .world for the world religion of the Antichrist.

8

China's Millions March

THE EMERGENCE of Red China as a powerful nation on the modern scene constitutes a very important development in events Scripture prophesies will take place at the end of the age. The sleeping giant, comprising more than 800,000,000 souls, is awakening and feverishly preparing to assume the role outlined for it in the prophetic Word.

"The point is," as Ross Terrill says, "that China so long the object of our policies and our judgments is no longer a passive but an active factor in the world."[1] Now the question that matters is not so much, What do we think of China? but, What does China think of us?

THE ORIENT AWAKES

China is not the only Asian nation enjoying a political and military awakening. All the countries east of the Euphrates River, asleep for centuries, are now arousing themselves to play a major role in world affairs. India, independent of British rule, is assuming a growing influence on the international scene.

Japan, in the half century preceding World War II, displayed the power an Oriental nation could become in a relatively short period once it adopted Western technology and ideas. Japan's defeat in World War II enabled China and India to come to the fore with increasing power in world politics.

Since World War II, Japan has not only recovered from defeat but has become a highly developed and wealthy industrial nation. Today she is exerting great influence in Asian affairs.

Lesser Asiatic nations are vying for places of recognition and are hoping to play larger roles in political events.

An awakened Orient, comprising a large part of the earth's land surface and the bulk of its population, is naturally to be expected to be vitally connected with end-time events. This fact would be true even if the prophetic Scriptures were silent on the place of the Orient in the consummating events of this age.

A REAL DRAGON APPEARS

No one nowadays believes in dragons. Nevertheless, a very real one has entered the modern arena. Red China is indeed a dreadful dragon, having more frightening potential for war and destruction than the Russian bear.

In less than three decades since the communist take-over, China has resolutely set out to become a world power. Her goal, however, is not peace. Violence and all-out war are the avowed means of destroying capitalism and the free world.

Mao Tse-Tung, who has ruled China for more than two decades, has never wavered from this concept which he considers to be the most fundamental principle of Marxist Leninism. He always has held that "Political power comes out of the barrel of a gun."[2] Under his regime, every effort has been made to develop war potential, particularly nuclear bombs and weapons.

In the decade or two ahead, the world will be faced with a fearful specter. An upsurging China, with vast human and material potential, constitutes a nuclear threat so terrifying that the nations of the free world dare spare no effort to anticipate it.

RED CHINA AND THE HOLY LAND

China is referred to in Scripture only indirectly. These references, however, are distinct and definite. Interestingly, they occur in connection with Palestine.

In Scripture, Israel is not reckoned among the nations (Num

23:9), but the nations are located with reference to Israel (Deu 32:8).

Accordingly, in the prophetic Word, China and other Asiatic powers are included under the caption "the kings of the east" (Rev 16:12). "The king of the north" alludes to Russia (Eze 39:2; Dan 11:40). "The king of the south" embraces Egypt and the Afro-Arabic nations (Dan 11:40). "The king of the west," though not actually so named, will be the head of the revived Roman empire.

A great military host, marshalled by "the kings of the East," no doubt headed by China, is seen invading the Holy Land at the end of the age in anticipation of the battle of Armageddon. The army is described in Revelation 9:16-19.

WHEN EAST MEETS WEST

God will use the hordes of Asiatic or Oriental peoples to effect great judgments that will be poured out upon the earth during the worldwide trouble that will precede the advent of Christ. The sixth trumpet of judgment announces a terrible woe (Rev 9:13-21).

A vast army of 200,000,000 from the Far East is loosed to march westward toward Palestine to overrun Israel. Up to this point, these Far-Eastern peoples have been divinely held back from the sphere of influence God has accorded Israel.

Now the divine restraint is removed. Four angels who are bound in the great river Euphrates are released (Rev 9:14). As ministers of judgment acting for God, these angels have been holding the eastern armies in check. Now they remove their restraint, so that the Asiatic military steamroller may advance westward to fulfill God's timetable in the age-end order of events.

In World War II, the Japanese navy almost brought an invasion army into the Middle East. With a powerful task force in the Indian Ocean and no obstacles standing in the way, the Japanese might have entered the African and Palestinian campaign and broken Allied resistance there. In fact, Admiral Yamamoto had already ordered the fleet to sail for the Red Sea. But for some inexplicable reason, the Japanese admiral reversed his order and turned the naval force around to head for the West Coast of the United States. American intelligence learned of the plan. The outcome was the battle of the Coral Sea, in which the Japanese were turned back in defeat.

Plainly, divine providence was at work. The time was not yet ripe for God to loosen the restraint imposed upon Asiatic peoples, permitting them to move westward and invade Israel. But that time will come! God Himself will reverse Rudyard Kipling's famous lines, "Oh, East is East and West is West — And never the twain shall meet."

The twain *shall* meet in the final clash for world supremacy.

THE EUPHRATES DRIES UP

The sixth angel, in a series of seven, pours out his bowl of divine wrath "upon the great river, Euphrates." As a consequence, its waters are "dried up, that the way of the kings of the east might be prepared" (Rev 16:12).

Whether the drying up of the Euphrates is construed as literal or symbolic, it speaks of the removal of this and every other barrier to the invasion of Palestine by the Asian confederacy.

In antiquity, before the era of modern engineering and mammoth bridge-building, this 1800-mile-long river presented a formidable obstacle to the westward march of ancient armies. It was scarcely fordable at any point, and effectively separated the East from the West.

The Euphrates River also constituted the eastern limit of the Roman empire, and moreover, it formed the northeastern boundary of the land promised to Israel by solemn covenant with Abraham (Gen 15:18; Deu 1:7; Jos 1:4). David conquered this territory, and his son Solomon ruled over it (1 Ki 4:21, 24). It will again be possessed by Israel when the kingdom is restored (Eze 47:13 — 48:35; Ac 1:6).

When the divine restraint is lifted so that the peoples of the Orient begin marching westward, every obstacle will be removed, as they sweep resistlessly toward the land of Israel.

A COLOSSAL ARMY WIPES OUT BILLIONS

How startling to the apostle John the enormous size of the invading Oriental army must have been. Two hundred million (Rev 9:16)! In John's day (ca. A.D. 90) this was more than the total population of the entire world.

Even in our day of population explosion, the number is colossal but not incredible. Present-day Red China significantly claims to have two hundred million men and women under direct or indirect military training.[a] Coincidentally this is the identical number of the invading Oriental contingent mentioned in Revelation 9:16.

From the brief but pointed prophetic allusion, the power and influence of the Orient in the final world war may be surmised.

Statesmen of the Western world from time to time have predicted the eventual awakening of the Orient and the threat of what used to be termed "the yellow peril." This threat will become a reality when China and her millions, augmented by other millions mustered by her Asiatic allies, will begin to march westward. The goal? To realize the godless communist dream of world conquest.

Although the army is wicked, it constitutes a scourge in God's hands to bring judgment upon lawless earth dwellers. This judgment is of such colossal magnitude that it staggers the imagination.

One third of the earth's population is destroyed by this military colossus (Rev 9:18). If the population of the world at the time were six billion, it would mean that two billion human beings would be wiped out at one time, according to this terrifying prophecy.

No doubt, on the natural plane, H-bombs and the latest thermonuclear weapons will play a large part in this horrifying destruction of human life. The fearful fact that Red China, by 1980 at the latest, will have ICBMs capable of delivering H-bombs "presents another grisly potential for fulfilling prophecy regarding this Oriental power."[4]

A Modern Army in Ancient Uniform

Scripture describes the Oriental army under the figure of an armored horse. In John's day there were of course no tanks or armored weapons, so the most formidable military weapon readily usable was an armored horse.

The seer envisioned "this future army in terms of the most

awesome and dreaded piece of military equipment that existed in his day."[5]

Each horse has a rider (Rev 9:16-18). The fire, smoke, and brimstone issuing from the horses' mouths evidently graphically symbolize destruction by modern weapons and chemicals under the figure of burning pitch or sulphur used by ancient armies. The army is further depicted as a poisonous serpent, bringing death in its wake.

A DEMONIZED ARMY WITH A GODLESS GOAL

The Oriental confederacy is inspired by the communist dream of world conquest. Dominated by Red China's tens of millions who have been systematically schooled in atheistic materialism with no god except the god of military power, the Asiatic horde determines to take over the earth.

Everyone who names the name of God or His Christ or who recognizes the Lord's possession of the earth will be a target for extermination and death. The Jew, by virtue of God's plan for the earth centering in him and the Jewish homeland as the hub of the earth in the coming kingdom, will be the special target for demonic hatred and attack.

Hence, in connection with the drying up of the Euphrates River that "the way of the kings of the east might be prepared" (Rev 16:12), John sees demon spirits going forth to enter "the kings of the earth and the whole world," to gather them to the battle of Armageddon (Rev 16:13-16).

Included in the terrible demonizing process of those days are not only the armies of the revived Roman empire of the West, but those also of the Asiatic confederacy advancing from the East. Though these two great future power blocs will oppose each other, they will be one in their mutual hatred of God and Christ and in their determination to thwart the divine purpose for the earth to be realized through the nation Israel.

For such a wicked purpose, demonic dynamic will be necessary and abundantly available. Beside the free demons that are now at work in the world (Eph 6:10-12; 1 Ti 4:1; 1 Jn 4:1-2) and will goad on the world's armies to the folly of Armageddon, millions of vicious depraved spirits, now imprisoned, will then be released from the "pit of the abyss," their present abode, to energize the unparalleled lawlessness of the end time (Rev 9:1-12).

THE SINO-SOVIET SPLIT

One of the extremely significant events of our day that has large prophetic import is the rift between Russian and Chinese Communism that grew during the sixties.

Astute students of international affairs, like George Kennan and numerous United States diplomats, were aware from the start that the Sino-Soviet tie was not secure or lasting.[6] The whole world watched as the divergence grew through the 1960s, until the final split came, which now is apparently irreparable.

In the light of Scripture, competent students of prophecy all along anticipated a rupture between Chinese and Soviet Communism. When God reduces Russia in the middle of the tribulation period, according to Ezekiel 38 and 39, the nations allied with the Soviet will be destroyed as well.

If China and other Asiatic confederates were allied with the Soviet Union at the time of the destruction of Russia, the Oriental powers would also be wiped out. In such a case it would be impossible for these Oriental powers to regain their strength to become a formidable antagonist of the last world dictator, the head of the revived Roman empire of the West.

DANIEL'S PREVIEW OF THE ORIENTAL INVASION

The prophet Daniel foresaw in panoramic view the end-time military invasion from the Orient in connection with Russia's invasion of Palestine. As the Russian military colossus threatens the annihilation of the Israeli nation, the Russian leader hears "tidings out of the east" (Dan 11:44). This news of the advance of the Oriental armies furnishes the occasion for his mad attempt to destroy Israel, which in turn results in his own destruction by divine intervention (see Eze 38-39).

Left in supreme power in the West, the head of Rome revived

(the Federated States of Europe) will now have to face the advancing armies from the East.

THE ASIATIC CONFEDERACY AND ARMAGEDDON

The kings of the East will march westward along the Fertile Crescent to challenge the claim of the head of the revived Roman empire to worldwide dominion. These two great power blocs will prepare for battle at Armageddon in the plain of Esdraelon in Palestine. Here East will meet West to determine who will rule the world.

As the greatest battle of all history is about to be fought, a most startling chain of events takes place. The sun is darkened, the moon will fail to give light, the stars will fall from heaven, and "the powers of the heavens shall be shaken" (Mt 24:29).

"And then shall appear the sign of the Son of man in heaven" (Mt 24:30). This is the outshining of God's glory emblazoning the heavens. In light more resplendent than the sun, the demon-driven armies of the world will behold the splendor of Him who is the rightful Possessor of the earth.

What will be the response of the kings and their armies poised to do battle with each other for possession of the earth?

Instantly, before the overpowering glory of a far superior foe, they will forget their mutual hostility. They will join together to repel what they recognize as an invasion from outer space.[7] They will sense that the rightful Possessor of not only earth but heaven (Gen 14:19) is moving in to take possession of that for which they had planned to war with one another to obtain.

HAIL THE RIGHTFUL CONQUEROR AND KING!

He will descend in clouds of glory. He will appear as irresistible Conqueror. By His spoken word He will slay the huge armies drawn up at Armageddon. In a moment He will annihilate the greatest display of military might this world has ever assembled (Rev 19:11-16).

East gathered against West will now join with the West against Him who appears as absolute King and Lord; these two evil powers will never use their weapons upon each other. Futilely they will turn them upon the Lord of glory. But they will find them powerless in the higher realm of the spiritual and the supernatural.

Not only will all munitions and weapons fail, the kings and their armies will be mowed down in death as the "sharp sword" that proceeds "out of his mouth" (Rev 19:15) speaks death to His foes as it speaks life to His own.

Doom of Chinese Communism

The seeds of atheistic, materialistic philosophy cannot be sedulously sown in the hearts of 800,000,000 Chinese people and the harvest not be catastrophic. Suffering and destruction unparalleled in human history are predestined for this evil. Untold millions have already been murdered to establish it. Uncounted millions will go down in destruction and death before its deadly career is cut off.

At Armageddon, Communism and every other false scheme of Satan and fallen man will be destroyed. The returning Christ is humanity's only hope.

9

Tribulation Engulfs the Earth

PEOPLE HAVE BECOME accustomed to looking at the future of the human race with serious misgivings. With phenomenal scientific and technological advance threatening man's undoing upon this planet, it is not impossible to envision an atomic holocaust that could annihilate the race and reduce the earth to a cinder.

With apparently irreconcilable differences existing between the nations of the world, the possibility of another global struggle presents a frightful prospect. A jittery generation may well ask, Will man survive? Will this generation be the last? Will man perish in a nuclear nightmare?

WORLDWIDE TROUBLE AHEAD

The prophetic Word, of course, envisions this era in world history. It was foreseen and described in detail by both Old and New Testament prophets.

Daniel declared it would be "a time of trouble, such as never was since there was a nation even to that same time" (Dan 12:1). Our Lord Himself emphasized its uniqueness and worldwide severity. He said it will be a time of tribulation, "such as was not since the beginning of the world to this time, no, nor ever shall be" (Mt 24:21).

Tribulation has been the common lot of God's people in every age. But this time of trouble will be unique in its fearful intensity and worldwide extent. It is therefore presented in Scripture as "the

105

great tribulation" (Rev 7:14, Greek). It will be a period of terrific trial that "shall come upon all the world, to try them that dwell upon the earth" (Rev 3:10).

It is quite evident that previous wars and calamities cannot be the great tribulation. They lack the intensity, worldwide scope, and age-end significance, which in Scripture are connected with this era.

Is the World Coming to an End?

People often get the notion that the approaching end of the age is the end of the world. The idea is quite widespread, since the term *age* is often rendered "world" in the King James Version and equated with the earth (e.g., Mt 13:39; 24:3; 28:20).

Indeed, one recent book on prophecy has captivated the popular imagination by employing the title, *The Late Great Planet Earth*.

Yet as devastating as the approaching world catastrophe will be, it is not really the end of the world. During this period, the earth will be visited by awful plagues and judgments. But this planet itself will not be destroyed nor mankind completely exterminated.

Billions will perish in the coming cataclysm. But a remnant will survive to enter the kingdom which Christ will set up on the earth at His second advent.

Why the Tribulation?

God has an important purpose in the coming period of world-wide trouble. During this time of judgment, He will weed out rebellious sinners and call out a redeemed people to populate Christ's millennial kingdom.

After the translation of the church, only unsaved people will be left behind on the earth. *All* the saved then living will be raptured to heaven.

The removal of the church will signal the beginning of what in the prophetic Word is known as "Daniel's seventieth week." This is the last seven-year period of Jewish history climaxing in the judgment of Israel and the nations, preparatory to the establishment of the kingdom at Christ's return (Dan 9:27).

In this dark hour when divine judgments sweep the earth, God in wrath will remember mercy. His Spirit will bring a multitude from among both Israel and the nations to a saving knowledge of Christ. Meanwhile, however, Israel and the nations will be judged for their rejection of Christ and their acceptance of the Antichrist.

In the coming world cataclysm, God will defend the name of His Son by executing His terrible wrath upon those who have rejected Him. In the fearful upheavals of that period of earth's anguish, He will demonstrate to the world that He alone is God and beside Him there is no other. He will show all men everywhere that Christ is absolute Lord and King over the earth.

ISRAEL IN DEEP TROUBLE

The return of the Jews to Palestine, eventuating in the establishment of Israel as a nation in 1948, constitutes one of the marvels of the twentieth century. It is a still greater marvel as foretold in the Scriptures. God's Word, all through the centuries of Israel's dispersion, has declared that the wandering Jew would one day return home.[1] Sincere students of the Word accordingly have always maintained it would happen. And it has happened!

But the Scriptures also declare that the Jews would return to their homeland to face the greatest crisis of anguish they have ever endured in their long history of suffering. In fact, the Israelis have been in a life-and-death struggle with Egypt and other Arab nations from the moment they set foot on Palestinian soil.

One noted columnist and TV commentator, reporting on the dilemma in the Middle East, describes Israel as "a nation in siege" surrounded by more than sixty million Arabs.[2] By contrast, Israel's own population is only 2,850,000, of which, startlingly enough, 350,000 are Arabs.

Yet, despite whatever Israel's present troubles may be, her greatest trial is yet future. It will come upon the nation in the terrible period of tribulation with which the age will end.

Bible prophecy indicates, in fact, that the tribulation, although it will be worldwide and affect all nations, will center in Israel. For this reason it is distinctively called "the time of Jacob's trouble."

Yet because the main purpose of it is to save and refine a nucleus of Jews to enter the kingdom, the prophet declares that Jacob shall "be saved out of it" (Jer 30:7).

Fearful will be the plight of the Jew in the vortex of the tribulation maelstrom. Jeremiah likens Israel's anguish to the pain of a woman in childbirth. Every face is blanched with pain (Jer 30:6).

Yet out of the ordeal, the Jewish people will be transformed from their unbelieving, scheming Jacob role to their regenerated character as Israel, a prince with God (Gen 32:32).

The apostle Paul sums up the grand finale. "And so all Israel shall be saved: as it is written, There shall come out of Sion the Deliverer, and shall turn away ungodliness from Jacob" (Ro 11:26).

Open the Seven-Sealed Book

The coming great tribulation will be the voice of God saying to Satan and wicked earth dwellers, "Squatters, get out!"

As a result of Adam's fall, man forfeited his rightful title to the earth, and Satan and wicked men have usurped control. In the end time they will attempt a complete take-over to drive the name of God and His Son from this planet.

But the rightful Owner of the earth is God's Son (cf. Ro 8:22-23; Eph 1:13-14; Rev 19:16). From a legal standpoint, the tribulation is His rising up to claim His rights, to oust Satan and wicked men from the earth, and to claim His possession.

Hence, Christ is seen opening the seven-sealed legal document, the title deed to the forfeited inheritance of the earth (Rev 5:1-10). He does this as "the lion of the tribe of Judah" (the royal tribe). As a kingly lion, He will tear His foes to pieces and assume His rightful title as "King of kings" (Rev 19:16; cf. Gen 49:8-10).

At His first advent, He appeared as the atoning Lamb "slain" (Rev 5:6). His death was the ground of redemption not only of sinners, but of the earth. At His second advent, however, He will appear as the conquering Lion, not slain by His enemies, but slaying His foes, and claiming what is rightfully His.

The seals He unlooses are the judgments He brings upon the earth to dispossess Satan and his lawless followers.

Loose the Seven Seals

The first seal introduces the scourge of the Antichrist. The second seal releases war and carnage. The third, famine; the fourth, pestilence and death (Rev 6:1-8).

The fifth seal heralds widespread persecution and martyrdom for those faithful to the Word of God in those awful days. The sixth seal signals earthquakes and commotions in the heavenly bodies (Rev 7:9-17).

The seventh seal concludes the opening of the seven-sealed book (Rev 5:1). Now the full contents of it can be released upon the earth and its wicked inhabitants in the terrifying trumpet and bowl judgments that follow.

Hide from the Wrath of the Lamb

The terrors of these tribulation judgments will be so severe that men in those days will say to the mountains and rocks, "Fall on us, and hide us from the face of him that sitteth on the throne, and from the wrath of the Lamb" (Rev 6:16).

Deluded and hardened by demonic powers released at that time from the abyss (Rev 9:1-12), men tormented by vicious spirits will "seek death and not find it." They will "desire to die, and death shall flee from them" (Rev 9:6).

Their cry will be, "The great day of [God's] wrath is come; and who shall be able to stand?" (Rev 6:17). But not one word of repentance shall come from their lips. Defiantly they will persist in their lawlessness and rebellion against God.

In that day God declares, "I will punish the world for their evil and the wicked for their iniquity; and I will cause the arrogancy of the proud to cease, and will lay low the haughtiness of the terrible. I will make a man more precious than fine gold" (Is 13:11-12).

"And they shall go into the holes of the rocks, and into the caves of the earth, for fear of the LORD, and for the glory of his majesty, when he ariseth to shake terribly the earth. In that day a man shall cast his idols . . . to the moles and to the bats; To go into the clefts of the rocks, and into the tops of the ragged rocks, for fear of the LORD, and for the glory of his majesty" (Is 2:19-21). The calamities and judgments of that day will bring man to the end of his rope. Those who will be saved and refined by these judgments shall cry: "Cease ye from man, whose breath is in his nostrils: for wherein is he to be accounted of?" (Is 2:22).

"And the loftiness of man shall be bowed down, and the haughtiness of men shall be made low: and the LORD alone shall be exalted in that day" (Is 2:17).

BLOW THE TRUMPETS OF JUDGMENT

The blowing of the first four trumpets results in severe disasters being visited upon the earth, the sea, the water supply, and the heavens (Rev 8).

The fifth trumpet releases a terrible judgment. The abyss is opened, and myriads of vicious demons, now imprisoned, are let loose to torment wicked earthdwellers and goad them on to gross idolatry and its attending sins of violence, occultism, sexual lawlessness, and thievery (Rev 9:1-12, 20-21).

The sixth trumpet presages a second colossal calamity. An Oriental army 200,000,000 strong advances westward to Palestine, wreaking terrifying destruction upon human life (Rev 9:13-19). The seventh trumpet announces a third terrifying judgment. This "woe" is said to come "quickly" and embraces all the remaining judgments, particularly the awful bowl judgments, prior to Christ's return and the setting up of His kingdom (Rev 11:14 — 20:3).

POUR OUT THE BOWLS OF WRATH

Seven of these bowls are poured out (Rev 16:1-21). Their contents symbolize the consummating judgments of God that complete the divine punishment of sinners and bring to an end the tribulation period. When the last bowl is poured out, the victorious Christ returns with the saints from heaven to take possession of the earth (Rev 16:1 — 19:16).

The last bowl accordingly fulfills the final legal provisions of the seven-sealed book. Satan and wicked men are now dispossessed from their control of the earth, and Christ, the rightful Ruler and Lord of all, is about to take control.

The first bowl is emptied upon the earth, focusing upon the empire of the Antichrist. A grievous ulcer is inflicted upon those who have renounced Christ by receiving the mark of the beast to worship the Antichrist.

The second bowl is poured out upon the sea, which is turned into blood. This evidently symbolizes the complete moral and spiritual putrefaction of godless society. The third bowl is similar, in that fresh waters are turned to blood, evidently indicating the thoroughgoing contamination of all sources of inspiration by lawless earth dwellers.

The fourth bowl brings horrible torture, as men are scorched as solar heat is increased. Sinners in frightful anguish blaspheme God, revealing their true character as dupes of Satan.

With the outpouring of the fifth bowl, impenetrable darkness engulfs the empire of the beast and his capital. Men gnaw their tongues in pain as they are fearfully tormented by demonic powers.

The outpouring of the sixth bowl witnesses the removal of every barrier that has held back "the kings of the east." As a result, the armies of China and the Orient, 200,000,000 strong, invade the West, bringing in their wake untold destruction and death.

The Final Stroke of God's Wrath

The pouring out of the seventh bowl brings the tribulation period to its terrible climax of judgment. This bowl is emptied "upon the air," the realm of Satan (Eph 2:2) and upon the earth where he is now operating. The devil, having previously been cast out of the heavenlies onto the earth (Rev 12:9), meanwhile, has been staging his last desperate and mad attempt to take over this globe, as he operates through the beast, the false prophet, and their followers.

Consummating the judicial wrath of God against Satan and demon-driven earth dwellers, the seventh bowl takes the form of a gigantic, globe-girdling earthquake followed by a plague of incredibly huge hailstones, as much as one hundred pounds in weight.

The violence of the earthquake and the hail shatters to pieces the evil institutions of men and utterly destroys the satanic world system of Babylon.

The cry from heaven, "It is done!" (Rev 16:17), dramatically announces upon earth the completion of the wrath of God upon those who have so wickedly refused the gracious cry of God's Son from the cross, "It is finished!" (Jn 19:30).

Will Mankind Destroy Itself?

With such catastrophes impending, one may well ask the question, Will men annihilate one another?

This dismal prospect is at least a possibility. In the light of man's phenomenal advance in the development of nuclear weapons of war capable of unimaginable destruction of life, the specter of the annihilation of vast sections of the human race haunts the minds of men. Scientists and military men who know the facts are fearful of the possibilities.

The United States has missiles that in a matter of minutes could dispatch nuclear warheads to any country of Europe, releasing more destructive power than in all the explosives employed in World War II. Russia most assuredly has the same capabilities. China is rapidly pressing toward the same frightful capability.

It is staggering to ponder the fact that men now have the potential to annihilate one another.

Many Bible students used to be skeptical that men could bring such widespread devastation upon the earth as is so graphically described in the book of the Revelation. But not any longer!

When one reads in the Apocalypse that under the sixth trumpet judgment one third of the earth's population is killed (Rev 9:18), no longer does the overwhelming immensity of the destruction of human life appear incredible. Imagine! Two billion people wiped out at one stroke, if the population at the time were six billion.

No wonder, God, speaking prophetically of the coming tribulation, declares: "And I will punish the world for their evil, and the wicked for their iniquity" (Is 13:11).

Does the Bible Prophesy Atomic War?

It seems possible, from numerous passages describing the terrors of the coming time of trouble, taken from both Old and New Testament prophets, that an atomic war is possible.

Isaiah, for example, speaks of "the day of the LORD . . . cruel both with wrath and fierce anger, to lay the land desolate" with God destroying "the sinners thereof out of it" (Is 13:9).

He foresees "the land utterly emptied" and "the inhabitants of the earth . . . burned and few men left" (Is 24:3, 6).

Jeremiah envisions "the slain of the LORD . . . at that day from one end of the earth even unto the other end of the earth . . . not lamented, neither gathered, nor buried" (Jer 25:33).

John foresees death riding a pale horse with hell following him killing "a fourth part of the earth" (Rev 6:8). He also sees "a great mountain burning with fire . . . cast into the sea" with the third part of the sea becoming blood (Rev 8:8), possibly a figurative representation of a huge atomic explosion, bringing death and destruction to a wide area.

John also sees what is apparently a huge Oriental army, equipped with nuclear weapons, wreaking horrible destruction as it advances westward to kill one third of earth's population (Rev 9:18).

These and other passages seem to suggest at least that atomic war will be employed during the tribulation period. But for several reasons such nuclear war will, of necessity, be controlled by God, if not by man.

Nuclear Holocaust and God's Prophetic Program

It is clear from Bible prophecy that man will not be wiped off the earth by destroying himself in an end-time nuclear holocaust. The reason is that God has a continuing purpose for the earth and for mankind on the earth.

At the end of the tribulation, according to the divine prophetic program, Christ will return to reign as absolute King and Lord in the coming age. If mankind succeeded in exterminating itself, there would be no one to receive Him or over whom He could reign. In such a case, God's prophetic program would collapse.

Hence it is necessary that a remnant of righteous people from both Israel and the nations, be preserved. Only in this way can Christ's purposes for this earth and the race be realized.

This preserved remnant will be redeemed. Some will turn to God during the tribulation judgments. Others apparently are redeemed after the tribulation in the intense evangelistic activity of saved Israelites brought into the kingdom (Zec 8:20-23). They will enter the kingdom as saved souls, but they will have unglorified bodies.

Tribulation Limited for the Elect's Sake

For this very reason of preserving a remnant, Christ foretold that the judgments of the tribulation would be so intense that if the period were not terminated, but men instead were permitted to continue indefinitely in their godless rebellion, the human race would be completely wiped out. "And except those days be shortened, there should no flesh be saved: but for the elect's sake those days shall be shortened" (Mt 24:22).

Our Lord did not mean that the period of the tribulation itself would be reduced from its established length. The prophet Daniel gives the exact length of the period as seven years. It is divided into two parts of three and one-half years, or forty-two months, or 1260 days.

Christ meant that the severe tribulation period is limited to 1260 days (Dan 7:25; 12:7; Rev 13:5; 19:9-20). If it went on longer, mankind — including the elect — would perish from the earth. God has set strict bounds on this era of awful judgment. His purpose is to preserve a remnant out of it, as He preserved Noah and his family out of the flood.

God's Wrath — Man's Judgment

It is significant to note that the vast devastation and worldwide destruction of life in the tribulation are *not* from men. They are from God upon men. God will use Satan, demons, and wicked men to effect these judgments. But the judgments themselves will be the Lord's, not man's. He who rules in heaven and is about to rule upon the earth will release these punishments upon godless, rebellious men.

Accordingly, it will not be some superpower like the United States, Russia, or China that will press a button to release some gigantic missile that will decimate millions of people and ravage a huge area, as Jeremiah envisioned.

The dead will be "the slain of the LORD" (Jer 25:33). The Lord Himself will release these terrors. He will be in control. It will be *His* judgment upon sinners to accomplish *His* purposes.

Also, it is to be noted that these judgments represent the outpouring of God's wrath, not man's.

When unrepentant sinners call for the rocks and the mountains to hide them, it is from "the wrath of the Lamb" they try to escape (Rev 6:16-17).

The worshipers of the beast drink of "the wine of the wrath of God" (Rev 14:9-10). In the seven awful plagues that consummate, the tribulation "is filled up the wrath of God" (Rev 15:1). The angels pour these "vials of the wrath of God" upon the earth (Rev 16:1).

Hence, if God permits men to use atomic warfare, it will be to accomplish His purpose and to glorify His name. The race cannot annihilate itself by atomic warfare, or otherwise.

The divine plan requires a remnant to survive in every age, including the tribulation. God is at the helm. He will be in absolute control in the darkest days ahead, when Satan, demons, and wicked men reach the zenith of rebellion against Him and seem about to take over control of the earth.

When man's blasphemy reaches its highest pitch and his noisy rebellion is most vocal, the solemn command will go forth: "Be silent, O all flesh, before the LORD: for he is raised up out of his holy habitation" (Zec 2:13).

WILL WORLD WAR III BREAK OUT BEFORE THE RAPTURE?

This question often arises in people's minds. Those who believe in a posttribulation rapture, of course, face the possibility of going through the nightmare of the coming time of trouble, including

Armageddon. Those who believe Christians will go through the first half of this period too face possible terrible eventualities.

But for the believer who is assured that the rapture will occur before the tribulation, the question is, Will another world war take place before that event?

Obviously no dogmatic answer to this question can be given, because Scripture furnishes no categorical declaration. However, a fairly definitive conclusion can be reached when the details of God's revealed prophetic program are correlated with conditions and developments as they exist in the world today.

"It is difficult," in the light of this comparison, as Dwight Pentecost aptly observes, "to see how the Lord can delay His coming to allow time for another world war with all the destruction it would entail."[3]

The reason for this conclusion is quite simple. The political, religious, and spiritual stage is now set for the events of the end time. Another world war would inevitably seriously disarrange the stage, and to rearrange it might take generations.

First, there exists today the political alignment that is predicted for the last days. Russia dominates the lands north of Palestine. The Arab states appear on the south, China and the Oriental nations on the east, and the Federated States of Europe on the west. Israel is back in the land, ready to play her important, predestined end-time role.

Second, the religious and ecclesiastical situation presages the fact that the end of the age is not far off. The great apostasy and the modern ecumenical movement are preparing Protestantism and Romanism for the merger into the harlot system of Revelation 17 and the one-world church of the tribulation period.

Last, the spiritual and moral conditions of our time cry out for divine judgment. Men are rejecting God's Word on a colossal scale. Lawlessness, occultism, immorality, and wickedness of every sort abound. God seems to be preparing the world for approaching judgment.

In the light of the stage set for the events of the end time, this judgment would seem to require the removal of God's people in the rapture and the loosing of the divine wrath upon the wicked and the rebellious in the coming great tribulation.

God's people are to look up "when these things begin to come to pass" for their redemption draws near (Lk 21:28).

The unsaved and the wicked, however, can only look around, their hearts "failing them for fear, and for looking after those things which are coming on the earth" (Lk 21:26).

10

The War That Ends War

AFTER TWO WORLD WARS in the twentieth century, beside innumerable localized conflicts, there is a deep-seated desire for peace among peoples of every nation.

President Nixon admirably expressed the sentiments of most Americans and men of goodwill everywhere: "Peace is our goal, and peace will be achieved in our time, but we hope peace that will live for a generation or longer."[1]

In the course of the same interview, President Nixon declared that to strive for this lasting peace was the reason for his trip to Peking and his then-projected visit to the Soviet Union. He also declared, "That is why we are trying to end the [Vietnam] war responsibly, in a way that would discourage those who would start wars, rather than encourage them."[2]

Wise and sober men cannot do otherwise than to commend the noble efforts and hopes of the President for lasting peace. However, the careful student of Bible prophecy knows very definitely that all such efforts and hopes, no matter how praiseworthy, will eventually prove futile. Scripture clearly indicates that increased tensions producing new hostilities among nations will inevitably erupt into the greatest war of all time, as the end of the age approaches.

WARS AND RUMORS OF WARS

Daniel, in his famous prophecy of the seventy weeks, declared that to the end of the age "shall be war; desolations are determined" (Dan 9:26, Hebrew).

Our Lord Himself, in His famous discourse to His disciples on

Mt. Olivet, declared: "Ye shall hear of wars and rumors of wars: see that ye be not troubled: for all these things must come to pass, but the end is not yet. For nation shall rise against nation, and kingdom against kingdom" (Mt 24:6-7a).

The apostle Paul warned that "The day of the Lord so cometh as a thief in the night. For when they shall say, Peace and safety; then sudden destruction cometh upon them as travail upon a woman with child; and they shall not escape" (1 Th 5:2-3).

No Peace Without the Prince of Peace

Despite the best efforts of diplomats and statesmen on behalf of peace, the strife that has embroiled the nations through the centuries will continue till Christ returns. The reason is twofold. The satanic world system that now prevails, with the devil and demonic powers free to operate, is characterized by greed, ambition, and struggle, which make permanent peace impossible (Ja 4:4).

Then, too, the rightful ruler of the earth, Jesus Christ, the Prince of Peace, is away. Not until He returns to destroy the satanic system and wicked men and set up His own earth rule, will lasting peace become a reality.

When Christ returns in glory, He will purge out the rebellious and the wicked from the earth. At the same time, Satan and his demon helpers will be consigned to the abyss (Zec 13:2; Rev 20:1-3). This cataclysmic event will not only terminate "the times of the Gentiles" when the nations have been in the ascendency and Israel trodden under their heel (Lk 21:24), it will also mark the collapse of the evil world system — that order and arrangement under which Satan has organized unbelieving mankind.

When Satan is taken out of the way, he will no longer be able to force his principles of selfishness and greed upon mankind. The cause of tensions and wars will be removed. Mankind under the firm but beneficent rule of the Prince of Peace will follow and enjoy peace.

Tribulation and the Tramp of Marching Armies

The coming cataclysmic end of the age, called in Scripture the tribulation, will witness the march of vast armies and the dramatic clash of huge military machines. Despite summit meetings, nuclear test ban agreements, and arms-limitations treaties, the end of the age will be characterized by military preparation unparalleled in scope in the history of mankind. The US-Soviet agreements on limiting strategic nuclear weapons will undoubtedly for a time, at least, curb the costly and dangerous arms race.[3] But world tensions inevitably will necessitate continued military buildups and crises that will eventually ignite the spark that will set off the final world war.

While the great nations are busy in joint interplanetary space exploration and travel, they will be vying for control of the earth.* The life-and-death struggle for this planet will demonstrate how unready unregenerate man is to live on other planets when he has not learned to live in peace with his fellowman on the earth.

The final great conflict between the nations, toward which mankind is headed, will eclipse anything recorded in the annals of human history. So intense and terrible will be this final war that the Bible's designation of it as "Armageddon" has become synonymous with conflict and slaughter that defy description.

The Focal Point of the Final War

Amazingly enough, the coming world holocaust will center not in Europe, Africa, or Asia, as strategic as these regions may be in world affairs today, but in the tiny land of Palestine. Armageddon will be a titanic tussle for the possession of the territory of the small but significant nation of Israel.

This fact may seem incredible, unless the basic nature of the end-time contest is comprehended. Armageddon will be a struggle for control of the earth. In its last stages, it will be men fighting against God. Hence, it will be energized by demon spirits "working miracles" (Rev 16:14).

These demonic spirits, who themselves are rebels against God, will inspire men to resist the divine plan to take over the earth. The

---

* Says NASA administrator James Fletcher, "I think that the first mission of U. S. and Russian astronauts will hardly be the last" ("Cooperation in the Cosmos," *Time* [June 5, 1972], p. 19).

clash will be with the returning Christ, who appears from heaven as absolute King and Lord to set up His earthly reign.

This theocratic rule will be exercised from Jerusalem, as the capital, through the nation Israel restored in millennial glory (Is 2:2-3). Satan and demonic powers fully realize this. Accordingly, in a mighty attempt to thwart the divine purpose, they will "go forth unto the kings of the earth and of the whole world" to bring them against Palestine and the city of Jerusalem (Rev 16:14; cf. Zec 12:1-10).

The inhuman cry of the demon-driven armies of Armageddon, will be; "On to Jerusalem! Annihilate the Jew! Defeat God's purpose! Take over the earth! Banish the name of God and of His Christ from this globe!"

"In that day shall the Lord defend the inhabitants of Jerusalem; and he that is feeble among them . . . shall be as David; and the house of David shall be as God, as the angel of the Lord before them" (Zec 12:8).

"In that day," declares the Lord, "I will seek to destroy all the nations that come against Jerusalem" (Zec 12:9).

Israel's Foes at Armageddon

Four great power blocs will advance against Israel in the series of conflicts that close the age and culminate in Armageddon. Hence these confederations of nations are designated in Scripture according to their general location with respect to Palestine and the nation Israel.

"The king of the north" (Russia and her allies), "the king of the south" (Egypt and the Pan-Arab bloc), and "the kings of the east" (China and the Oriental alignment), play major roles in the last great war.

"The king of the west," though not actually so specifically designated in the Bible, is clearly the revived Roman empire, comprising the Federated States of Europe (Dan 2:34-35).

The fact that the divine allocation of the nations at the end time is based on their geographical relation to the nation Israel makes it obvious why for students of the prophetic Scriptures the establishment of the Israeli state in 1948 constituted an event of unparalleled importance.

Prior to World War II, Israel had no existence as a separate nation among the nations of the earth. Before the birth of modern Zionism in the last decade of the nineteenth century and the beginnings of Jewish settlement of Palestine in the twentieth century, the Jews were a homeless people, scattered among the nations of the earth. Their predicted end-time role in world history seemed incredibly remote, if not impossible.

But with the growth of Zionism and the return of the Jews to Palestine, the stage is gradually being set for the events of Armageddon.[4] From a mere 90,000 in 1914, the Jewish population of Palestine increased to 108,000 in 1925 and to 300,000 by 1935. Hitler's persecution of the Jews led to the greatest influx of Jewish immigration, which has continued at a rapid rate since World War II.

Today Israel has a population pushing toward three million. With an expanding economy bolstered by a thriving tourism, the country is in the process of becoming the strategic and economic prize that will eventually lure the four great power blocs of the world to Armageddon in a titanic struggle to get possession of Palestine.

Armageddon — Phase 1

Although the Bible presents the main features of the final world conflict, it does not supply much detail. As a result, the time and sequence of certain events are subject to inference and, in some instances, to speculation. Prophetic scholars, accordingly, differ to some degree on the various phases of the final age-end war.

Apparently the spark that ignites World War III, as shown in chapter 7, is a Pan-Arab attack on Israel. Daniel glimpsed the fact that the intense hatred of the Arabs for the Israelis would one day explode into the final conflict, unleashing the red horse of war (Rev 6:4).

"At the time of the end" the prophet declared, "shall the king of the south [Egypt and the Arab nations] push at him [the Israeli leader]" (Dan 11:40). This leader will apparently be an unregenerate Jew in Palestine in league with the head of the revived Roman empire.

ARMAGEDDON — PHASE 2

The invasion of Palestine from the south by the Pan-Arab coalition will immediately trigger a second invasion from the north by Russia and her satellites. As noted in chapter 7, this fact becomes apparent as the result of a correct interpretation of Daniel 11:40-46.

That this invasion constitutes an initial phase of Armageddon is made clear by Daniel. "At the time of the end," he specifies, "the king of the north [Russia]" shall come against the Israeli leader in a gigantic amphibious and land attack, overrunning Palestine and the Near East and sweeping down into Egypt (Dan 11:40-43).

That this maneuver means that Russia, in the final showdown, will double-cross Egypt and the Pan-Arab states, has been demonstrated in chapter 7. To realize her vaulting ambition to dominate the world's sea-lanes, Russia will realize she must destroy Arab as well as Jew. As she hastens back to consolidate her claim upon Palestine and to annihilate the Israeli nation, she is supernaturally and catastrophically destroyed (Eze 38:4; Dan 11:45).

ARMAGEDDON — PHASE 3

The annihilation of the Russian military machine, with the neutralization of the United Arab and African armies, completely upsets the balance of power among the nations at the end time. Only two great power blocs remain — the combined armies of the Western world, confederated under the Roman leader (the Antichrist), and the vast armies of the Orient, apparently mustered under the leadership of Red China.

With the fall of Russia, the Roman dictator will reign supreme in the Western hemisphere. He becomes the head of a world empire like ancient Rome (Rev 13:1-10). With the false prophet, he will proclaim a demon-energized message to the non-Oriental world. His call will persuade the nations of the whole earth (exclusive of the Oriental bloc) to send contingents to the Near East to destroy the sole remaining great war machine on earth (Rev 16:13-14).

Undoubtedly his appeal will be made with glowing promises of peace once the war-mongering communist forces of the Orient are wiped out. In response, "the kings of the earth and the whole world" will dispatch units to the Middle East to fight under the Antichrist's command against the advancing "kings of the east" (Rev 16:12, 14). No doubt, the United States of America will be represented with the United States of Europe and other nations of the Western world, including South America, Africa, and Australia.

The armies of the Antichrist will be assembled for battle at Armageddon. This is the plain of Esdraelon, which extends across the Holy Land from Haifa, on the Mediterranean, to the Jordan River, being approximately fourteen miles wide and twenty miles long (Rev 16:16). Here the immense conflict will center.

But the entire land of Palestine and surrounding areas will also be involved in the terrific clash between the armies of the West and the East.

Another focal point is the valley of Jehoshaphat east of Jerusalem (Joel 3:2, 12), as well as the city of Jerusalem itself (Zec 12:2-10; 14:2-3). Also mentioned is the land of Edom (Is 34:1-6; 63:1-6). So widespread is the carnage that, it is said, "Blood flowed out of the wine press, so that for two hundred miles it came up to the horses' bridles" (Rev 14:20, Berkeley).

What a revelation of the wide extent and unimaginable horror of this final conflict! Man struggling with man for possession of the earth! Palestine overrun with armies from its length to its breadth! Humanity sounding its own death knell and about to destroy itself, unless the Lord intervenes.

ARMAGEDDON — PHASE 4

The most amazing thing about Armageddon is its outcome. When the armies of the world are locked in devastating conflict and mankind threatens to annihilate itself, God will intervene and Christ will return. As East and West fight for the control of the earth, suddenly the rightful Owner and Lord of the earth and the universe serves notice that He is about to assume control.

Suddenly the sun and moon will be darkened and, "The stars

will fall from the sky and the forces of heaven will be shaken" (Mt 24:29, Berkeley). The earth, too, will reel like a drunkard, as "such a tremendous earthquake as had never occurred since man existed on the earth" levels "the cities of the nations" (Rev. 16:18-19, Berkeley) and effects far-reaching topographical changes in Palestine (Zec 14:4-5).

More terrifying to the embattled armies at Armageddon than the shaking of the heavens and the earth will be the manifested presence of Deity. Terror will grip the hearts of demon-driven men, as the heavens so recently shaken now blaze with the splendor of Deity that outshines the sun.

Jesus Himself spoke of this in His discourse concerning His second advent, "Then will the sign of the Son of Man be shown in the sky, and all the tribes of earth will mourn" (Mt 24:30, Berkeley).

The Shekinah glory, that hovered over the mercy seat and appeared in the pillar of cloud by day and the pillar of fire by night that guided God's people through their wilderness journey, will emblazon the heavens.

Before He actually arrives, the Lord Jesus will reveal His glory to the earth. The sign will be recognized even by the apostate leaders gathered with their armies at Armageddon. They will sense that God is moving in to judge them. Dreadful terror will grip them, as the awful fact dawns upon them that they now face a mutual foe far greater than each other.

Quickly the leaders of both sides call for a cessation of hostilities toward one another. In haste they join forces against an invasion from outer space, that, unless checked, will prove disastrous to both.

John, the apostle, glimpsed this dramatic development. "Then I saw the beast and the kings of the earth and their armies mustered to wage war against the One mounted on the horse and against His army" (Rev 19:19, Berkeley).

Christ's Advent and the Climax of Judgment

That the armies of earth will turn from fighting one another to war against God demonstrates the depth of their delusion. What ridiculous folly to imagine that finite man can fight against the infinite God and win!

No wonder the psalmist, in the light of the folly of Armageddon, declares, "He who dwells in heaven laughs: the LORD derides them" (Ps 2:4, Berkeley).

Then the emblazoned heavens open and the all-conquering Christ appears. His victory is signaled by His riding upon a white horse. "On white horses," as sharing his victory, and "clothed in fine linen," as redeemed by His blood, "the heavenly armies follow Him" (Rev 19:14, Berkeley).

Earth's mightiest armaments are no match for this celestial host of redeemed and glorified men, led by Him whose name is "The Word of God" (Rev 19:13, Berkeley). He merely speaks, and His word is like a sharp sword by which He slays His foes and smites the nations (Rev 19:15).

He who is called "Faithful and True," because He was "faithful" to death to redeem fallen mankind and because He is "the true God, and eternal life" (1 Jn 5:20), at this climactic moment, "justly . . . judges and wages war" (Rev 19:11, Berkeley).

Every right is His to possess the earth and to purge out the wicked and the rebellious. This He does as "He treads the wine press of the furious wrath of God the Almighty." Because man's iniquity reaches its utmost pitch at Armageddon, it merits and there receives the full measure of the divine displeasure.

PEACE AT LAST

Armageddon will be the war that ends war, because the Victor in that colossal conflict will be the mighty Christ who alone has the right to rule and who comes to exercise that rule as absolute Lord and King. Therefore, the apocalyptic seer notes that "On His robe and on His thigh He has His name inscribed: King of kings and Lord of lords" (Rev 19:16, Berkeley).

Peace will follow in His train because He roots out everything that causes war — sinners of every walk of life, the beast, the false prophet, and Satan and the demonic forces. The latter are consigned to the abyss (Rev 20:1-3). The beast and false prophet are cast alive into Gehenna, the lake of fire (Rev 19:19-20). The rebellious armies embattled at Armageddon (Rev 19:17-18), as well as all other rebels throughout the earth, are "put to death with the sword that issued from the mouth" of the omnipotent Conqueror (Rev 19:21, Berkeley).

The outcome of Armageddon will demonstrate to every intelligent creature on earth that Jesus Christ is Lord and rightful Ruler, mankind's only hope for peace and a warless world.

11

Christ Returns to Judge Sinners

THE GREAT CLIMACTIC PROPHECY of the book of the Revelation is the second advent. As Christ returns to earth as absolute King and Lord, judgment is declared to be an important feature of His coming. "In righteousness He judges and wages war" (Rev 19:11, NASB). His waging war actually is also a vital part of His judging, for it is He who by the omnipotent word of His mouth decimates the demon-driven hordes at Armageddon (Rev 19:15).

But Armageddon is only the beginning of Christ's role as Judge in connection with the events that accompany the second advent. As He strikes death to His impious foes embattled against Him in a mad attempt to thwart His take-over of the earth, He must yet deal with rebels and sinners in the nonmilitary population of the world.

This judgment will involve all humanity in two distinct categories — Jews and non-Jews (Gentiles). This division of mankind figures very prominently in this judgment, because Christ returns to set up His kingdom over Israel (Ac 1:6). The issue will be who out of Israel, primarily, and, secondarily, who out of the Gentiles will qualify to enter the kingdom.

WHAT IS THE KINGDOM CHRIST WILL SET UP?

Christ's kingdom is foretold in great detail and prominence by Old Testament prophets. This kingdom is to be realized by the descendants of Abraham through Isaac and Jacob (Israel). It is also predicted to be Davidic and to be set up under David's heir, who is to be virgin born, therefore, truly Man (Is 7:13-14; 11:1). At the same time, He is to be "The mighty God, The everlasting Father [the eternally existing One], The Prince of Peace" (Is 9:6-7; Jer 23:5; Ho 3:4-5). Hence He is to be God incarnate (Zec 13:7).

The kingdom itself is to be heavenly in origin and administration (Dan 2:34-35, 44-45). However, it is to be set up on the earth, with Israel as its chief nation and the city of Jerusalem as its capital (Is 2:2-4; 4:3-5; 24:23; 33:20; 62:1-7; Jer 23:5; Joel 3:16-17).[1]

The kingdom, moreover, is to be established first, over regathered, restored, and converted Israel at Christ's second advent (Is 11:11 — 12:6; 35:1-10; 60:1-22; Jer 23:5-8; 30:7-11; Eze 20:33-40; Joel 3:1, 16-17). Then it is to spread over the earth and become universal (Ps 2:6-8; 22:27-31; Zec 9:10; 14:16-19).

Righteousness and peace will prevail in the new order (Ps 72:1-10; Is 11:4-9). Equity and justice will be enforced (Is 9:7). Flagrant sin will be visited with instant punishment, for Christ will rule with a rod of iron (Ps 2:9-12; Is 11:4-5). Preflood longevity apparently will be restored (Is 65:20; Zec 8:4). Great prosperity and blessing from God will be enjoyed, as the vast majority of earth's population will be saved and in willing submission to Christ and those associated with Him in millennial administration.

JUDGMENT MUST PRECEDE KINGDOM BLESSING

Since the kingdom will represent a rigid rule of righteousness under Christ's administration, it will be necessary to purge out the rebellious and unrepentant. Whether this purging will involve all the unregenerate of the age of moral and spiritual accountability or merely those who were openly rebellious, such as those who submitted to the Antichrist and received his mark, is not certain.

Some prophetic scholars are of the opinion that "the millennial kingdom will begin with the entire adult population of the world limited to those who have put their faith in Christ."[2] The millennial age is conceived as "a new beginning comparable to that following the flood when Noah and his immediate family formed the entire population of the earth."[3]

Whatever degree the purging out will assume, the separation of the righteous from the unrighteous is a necessary prelude to the millennial kingdom. Our Lord declared there would be "two men in the field; one will be taken" in judgment, the other "will be left" to enter the kingdom. "Two women will be grinding at the mill; one will be taken" in death, the other "left" as a survivor to enjoy kingdom blessing (Mt 24:40-41).

Our Lord also anticipated the prekingdom judgment of those living when Christ returns to the earth to set up His righteous rule. The tares would then be separated from the wheat (Mt 13:37-42) and the bad fish from the good fish (Mt 13:47-50).

Our Lord Himself declared that at the end of the age preceding the kingdom, "The Son of Man will send forth His angels, and they will gather out of His kingdom all stumbling-blocks, and those who commit lawlessness, and will cast them into the furnace of fire; in that place there shall be weeping and gnashing of teeth" (Mt 13:41-42, NASB).

With the wicked removed, it is said, "Then the righteous will shine forth as the sun in the kingdom of their Father" (Mt 13:44, NASB).

Israel Judged Before Kingdom Blessing

The victorious Christ returning to earth will first deal in judgment with His elect nation Israel. This is to be expected, since the kingdom is first to be established over the descendants of Abraham. As the recipients of the covenants and promises of God (Ro 9:5), Israel has been guaranteed national regathering, conversion, and kingdom blessing under her Messiah-Redeemer and King (Deu 30:1-10). Her assured status in the coming age will be "the head" of the nations, not "the tail" (Deu 28:13).

But to be admitted to the kingdom, individual Israelites must be regenerated. Jesus was merely summarizing what the Old Testament prophets had taught, when He declared to Nicodemus, "You must be born again" (Jn 3:7, NASB). Apart from the new birth, our Lord insisted, one cannot "see" nor "enter into the kingdom of

God" (Jn 3:3, 5, NASB). "Are you [Nicodemus] the teacher of Israel, and do not understand these things?" (v. 10).

Hence when Christ returns, He must cause Israel as well as all humanity to pass under His judgment. This is a necessity. He must remove the rebel by death and cast out the unbeliever "into the outer darkness" (Mt 8:12; 22:13; 25:30, NASB). Before He can establish His kingdom, He must root out all opposition to His reign.

WISE AND FOOLISH VIRGINS

Israel's judgment at Christ's advent in glory takes place just prior to the establishment of Messiah's kingdom. "Then the kingdom of heaven will be comparable to ten virgins, who took their lamps, and went out to meet the bridegroom" (Mt 25:1, NASB). The ten virgins represent the nation Israel at the end of the tribulation period just before Messiah's appearance. The five wise virgins symbolize the believing remnant, who not only had a witness for God as Israelites (lamps), but were regenerated, Spirit-indwelt witnesses. They had oil in their vessels with their lamps (Mt 25:1-5).

The five foolish virgins symbolize the unbelieving segment of the nation. They only profess to look for Messiah's kingdom. Lacking oil in their flasks for adequate testimony to God's saving grace through Christ, they will be excluded from the Messianic rule about to be set up (Mt 25:6-10).

Jesus, in lauding the humble faith of the Gentile centurion, whose servant He healed, declared that "many [saved Gentiles] shall come from east and west, and recline at table with Abraham, and Isaac, and Jacob, in the kingdom of heaven; but the sons of the kingdom" (that is, Israelites to whom it was promised and to whom it uniquely belonged), "shall be cast out into the outer darkness" (Mt 8:11-12, NASB).

GOOD AND BAD SERVANTS

Israel's judgment at Christ's glorious advent and kingdom will not only test inner faith and heart salvation, as revealed in the parable of the ten virgins, it will also examine outward conduct as manifested in service for Christ and consequent reward, as portrayed in the parable of the talents (Mt 25:14-30).

The "man about to go on a journey, who called his own slaves, and entrusted his possessions to them" (Mt 25:14, NASB) represents Christ during His absence from the earth. His servants (slaves) portray Israel during the tribulation period. The five-talent and the two-talent servants speak of truly regenerated believers, faithful in service and witness. Each demonstrated his faithfulness by doubling his trust.

Each will receive commendation and reward from Christ, the Judge: "Well done, good and faithful slave; you were faithful with a few things, I will put you in charge of many things, enter into the joy of your master" (Mt 25:21, 23, NASB).

The one-talent servant who harshly accused his master of being hard and unjust, and who hid his trust in the ground, stands for an unsaved mere professor. He manifested his lost condition by his attitude and conduct toward his Lord. He is excluded from the kingdom and cast "into the outer darkness" (Mt 25:24-30).

Gentiles Judged Before Kingdom Blessing

After Christ has dealt with Israel, He will turn in judgment to the Gentiles. "He will sit on His glorious throne. And all nations will be gathered before Him" (Mt 25:31-32, NASB).

The place of this judgment is earth, not heaven. The throne, moreover, is not the Father's throne in heaven, which Christ now occupies (Rev 3:21). It is rather His own earthly millennial throne foretold by the Old Testament prophets (cf. 2 Sa 7:16). Jeremiah declared the time would come when the Lord would raise up "a righteous Branch" from the Davidic line, and "a King" who would execute justice and righteousness in the millennial earth from this throne (Jer 23:5).

The subjects of this judgment are declared to be "all nations" (Mt 25:32). The connotation is not political entities or countries, but "all Gentiles" in an individual sense. The Greek word *ethne* often means Gentiles, or the non-Jewish population of the world. The distinction in this instance, as the context clearly shows, is to

Jews who have just been judged. Now Christ the Judge must judge the non-Jewish peoples of the world on the eve of His setting up His kingdom.

The subjects of this adjudication will not only be Gentiles in distinction to Jews, they will be "all Gentiles" who are living on the earth at that time. The parallel is the preceding judgment of Israel representing all Jews living on the earth during the same climactic period of redemptive history.

Separating the Sheep from the Goats

With "all Gentiles" gathered before His throne, Christ will "separate them from one another, as the shepherd separates the sheep from the goats; and He will put the sheep on His right, and the goats on the left" (Mt 25:32-33, NASB).

According to Oriental custom, the right hand is the place of honor, privilege, and reward, while the left hand the place of separation (cf. Gen 48:13-20).

Sheep in Scripture metaphorically describe the Lord's regenerated people (cf. Ps 23; Jn 10:14-16). Jesus declared, "I am the good shepherd, and know my sheep, and am known of mine" (Jn 10:14). Goats, on the other hand, prefigure the unregenerate, who have never trusted Christ as Saviour (cf. Lev 16:8-9, 20-23).

To the sheep (the regenerate) on His right hand, the King shall say, "Come, ye blessed of my Father, inherit the kingdom prepared for you from the foundation of the world" (Mt 25:34). Saved Gentiles then living upon the earth, thus congratulated, will take their place under the rule of Christ to fulfill God's purpose. The earth, as the arena where the great contest between God and Satan will be staged, will witness in the coming kingdom God's complete triumph over the powers of darkness, according to a plan laid when God created the universe and laid the cornerstone of the earth (Job 38:4-7).

To the goats (the unregenerate and rebellious) on His left hand, the King will say, "Depart from me, ye cursed, into everlasting fire, prepared for the devil and his angels" (Mt 25:41). Unsaved Gentiles then living upon the earth, thus condemned, will be removed by death. Their soul and spirit, consigned to hades, will eventually be cast into Gehenna after the judgment for their works at the great white throne, following the kingdom age (Rev 20:11-15).

Our Lord's words concerning the fate of the unsaved in departing into "everlasting fire" are in a sense anticipative. Those unsaved previous to the great white throne do not go immediately into Gehenna at death. He speaks in this manner, however, because the physical death of the unregenerate necessitates the second death, which is eternal separation from God in Gehenna, the lake of fire (Rev 20:14).

THE KING ACKNOWLEDGES HIS BROTHERS

One of the most astonishing features of the judgment of Gentiles living at the time of Christ's advent in glory and the establishment of His earthly kingdom is the prominent reference to a class described by the Lord as "my brethren." Even more astonishing is our Lord's personal identification with this group, so eloquently emphasized in the New American Standard Bible.

"Then the king will say to those on His right, 'Come, you who are blessed of My Father, inherit the kingdom prepared for you . . . For I was hungry, and you gave Me something to eat; I was thirsty, and you gave Me drink; I was a stranger, and you invited Me in; naked, and you clothed Me; I was sick, and you visited Me; I was in prison, and you came to Me.'

"Then the righteous will answer Him, saying, 'Lord, when did we see You hungry, and feed You, or thirsty, and give You drink? And when did we see You a stranger, and invite You in, or naked and clothe You? And when did we see You sick, or in prison, and come to You?'

"And the King will answer and say to them, 'Truly I say to you, to the extent that you did it to one of these brothers of Mine, even the least of them, you did it to me'" (Mt 25:34-40, NASB).

Who are these whom Messiah the King so dramatically claims as His brothers? They are Jews saved by the preaching of "the gospel of the kingdom" after the rapture of the church (Mt 24:14).

During the tribulation period, God will sovereignly call and save 144,000 Jews (Abraham's descendants through Jacob, Rev 7:1-8).

Coming into fellowship with the crucified, risen, and glorified Christ, they will become powerful preachers of the gospel of salvation by grace through faith centering in the returning King and His kingdom to be set up on the earth. These zealous Jewish witnesses will have the same glorious ministry that the apostle Paul had in his day. This is what the apostle had reference to when he alluded to himself as "one untimely born" (1 Co 15:8, NASB). I believe he meant that he, as a fervent Jewish convert to Christ, was born before the era when there would be 144,000 other Jews, like himself, converted to Christ and zealously proclaiming Christ's salvation to the ends of the earth.

So glorious and wonderful will be the ministry of the 144,000 saved Jews and so faithful will be their powerful testimony, the King on His throne of glory will not be ashamed to call them "My brothers." More than that, He will consider Himself so intimately united to them that what was done or not done to them is the same as being actually done or not done to Himself.

The King's Brothers Acknowledge the King

The fact that the Lord's brothers endured hunger, thirst, homelessness, nakedness, sickness, and imprisonment suggests their fidelity to their newfound Saviour and Lord. They proved their willingness to suffer for Him amid the terrible persecutions and trials of the tribulation through which they passed. They proved their loyalty to their King. He attests His identity with them.

During the first three and one-half years of the tribulation, these witnesses will be allowed to preach unhindered. However, in the middle of the period, the Antichrist, who will head the revived Roman empire in the west, will attempt to stop the preaching of the gospel of the kingdom.

The emphasis on the King coming to set up His earthly kingdom will be an insufferable offense to him who himself aspires to be God and world king (2 Th 2:4). In proud rage he imposes a strict ban on gospel preaching and launches a diabolically cruel persecution against "the saints" (Rev 13:7).

Through his chief minister of economics and culture, he will institute a system to weed out all opposition to his godless plan of a one-world religion by which to dominate mankind. To attain his goal, he will issue a decree requiring everyone to swear loyalty to him and receive his mark to buy or sell. Those who will not submit, as will be the case of the Jewish witnesses, will be unable to buy food (Rev 13:17).

This is the reason the Jewish witness will suffer hunger and thirst. They will be homeless because their property will be confiscated. Even the clothes they wear will be taken from them. Such rigors will induce physical weakness and sickness. All these woes will be aggravated by imprisonment by the agents of the beast, who will institute an empire-wide spy system.[4]

But the grand thing is that those whom the Lord owns as His brothers before the throne of His millennial glory have faithfully owned Him through the agony of persecution, through which they have passed. No wonder the King views the treatment they received at the hands of their friends and foes as treatment accorded Him! To their friends and benefactors, and therefore friends of His also, come the glorious words, "Truly, I say to you, to the extent that you did it to one of these brothers of Mine, even to the least of them, you did it to Me" (Mt 25:40, NASB).

To their foes and persecutors, and therefore His foes also, issue the ominous words, "Truly I say to you, to the extent that you did not do it to one of the least of these, you did not do it to Me" (Mt 25:45, NASB).

WHY DO THE SHEEP ENTER INTO ETERNAL LIFE?

The King calls the "sheep" the "righteous" and declares they "go . . . into eternal life" (Mt 25:46, NASB) and, as the blessed of the Father, "inherit the kingdom" (v. 34). But the question is why?

On the surface it would appear that they are saved because of good works. They fed the hungry, gave drink to the thirsty, were hospitable to sojourners, clothed the naked, and visited the sick and the imprisoned. But salvation by works cannot be inferred here, as it is nowhere taught in God's Word. Men in every age are saved by grace through faith. This is the only way any member of Adam's fallen race can be brought out of spiritual death into eternal life.

The sheep on the right hand of the Judge are not *saved* because they fed, clothed, housed, and visited God's servants; they did these things *because* they were saved. This is not salvation by works, but salvation evidenced by works. They were justified before God, who sees the heart, by faith (Ro 3:28; 4:2-3). They were justified before men, who cannot see the heart, by works (Ja 2:21).

The omniscient Judge pronounces His decision on the basis of the latter principle, because He would justify the righteous before their persecutors, foes, and phoney imitators. He does so also to demonstrate the genuine character of their deeds as evidencing the fact that they were truly regenerated. But since it is not always true that a philanthropic and altruistic spirit manifests a regenerated heart, this problem is solved by the peculiar circumstances which form the background of the judgment.

It must be remembered that the people who are being judged are non-Jews who have survived the terrible sufferings of the great tribulation. This period is distinctively "the time of Jacob's trouble" (Jer 30:7) and will witness an unprecedented outburst of anti-Semitism. Doubtlessly throughout the world, but especially in the state of Israel, the Jewish people will be violently persecuted and killed (Mt 24:15-22).

Satan and demonic forces will realize that Christ's imminent advent and kingdom will spell their imprisonment in the abyss (Zec 13:2; Rev 20:1-3) and their eventual eternal doom (Rev 20:10). As a result, they will operate through the Antichrist, the false prophet, and their followers to utterly destroy the Jews in whom Messiah's kingdom centers and through whom His purposes for the earth will be consummated (Rev 13:7; 16:13-16). To destroy Israel will be considered as being tantamount to nullifying God's plan for man and the earth.

Under these special circumstances, anyone who would befriend the Jews, especially the 144,000 zealous Jewish witnesses, would be a marked man. Showing the simplest kindness to them, such as visiting them in prison, "when according to government edict they were to be hounded to death, would inevitably reveal a confidence in the Scriptures and in God."[5]

Such conduct, under these appalling conditions, becomes very significant. It indicates that the performer is motivated by the realization that the Jewish people are indeed God's elect people and that their Messiah is the Saviour of all who trust in Him. One who would so risk his life to render such kindnesses to a doomed people would inevitably be a believer in the Lord Jesus Christ.

Why Do the Goats Go Away Into Eternal Punishment?

The King calls the "goats" "accursed ones" and issues the command, "Depart from Me . . . into eternal fire" (Mt 25:41, NASB). The question again, as in the case of the sheep is, why?

Again on the surface it would seem that they are not saved because they failed to perform good works. They did not feed the hungry, give drink to the thirsty, or do other acts of kindness as the sheep did. But the goats did not do these things because they were *not* saved, as the sheep did them because they *were* saved.

Once more this is not salvation by works, but salvation *not* evidenced by works. The omniscient Judge renders His verdict on this ground because He would plainly show the unsaved their just condemnation before those whom they hated and persecuted.

As the sheep survived the horrors of the great tribulation, so will the goats. Both faced the same circumstances of reacting toward the violent anti-Semitism of the world government of the day. The sheep reacted in such a manner that they displayed their faith in Christ and His brothers, the Jewish people; the goats reacted in such a way that they revealed their unbelief and unregenerate condition.

With the separation of the sheep from the goats, the stage is set for Christ's millennial reign. To this golden age of peace and righteousness, a war-weary world may look forward with confidence and hope.

12

God's Great Society Established

FROM THE BEGINNING of human history, men have dreamed of an ideally perfect social order. Through the fog of inequalities, injustices, hostilities, and poverty, which sin has caused to settle upon the fallen human family, men here and there have glimpsed the dawn of a better day.

Such a golden age was envisioned by Hebrew seers, such as Isaiah (11:4-6; 12:1-3; 35:1-10) and Jeremiah (23:5-6). Ancient Greek philosophers too hoped for a better society. Plato, in his *Republic,* pictures a happy social order when men would abound in knowledge and wisdom. Augustine, the Christian theologian, in *The City of God,* wrote of the peace and prosperity that would girdle the earth when Christ reigns supreme. John Calvin's theocracy at Geneva furnishes an instance of man's hope to realize on earth the golden age predicted by the prophets.

One of the best known examples of an imaginary place pictured as having a perfect political social setup is found in Sir Thomas More's *Utopia* penned in 1516. Although published over four and a half centuries ago, it deals with practically all of the important social problems that plague society today. Few books better illustrate Lowell's description of a classic as "a commentary on the morning paper" than this famous work.[1]

THE AMERICAN DREAM

Perhaps no nation in history has had a greater opportunity than America to realize a social and political utopia, if such were attain-

139

able by man's efforts. Nowhere else in the world has a firmer foundation of freedom and justice been laid for building such an order. Nowhere else has the dream of a "great society" had more money and effort expended on it or excited more hope of attainment.

Under the Johnson administration, this trend seemed to rise to a grand crescendo. The Eighty-ninth Congress alone passed twenty-one new health programs, seventeen new educational programs, fifteen new economic-development programs, twelve programs for the cities, seventeen new resource-development and four new man-power-training programs.

These and other almost feverish legislative attempts to alleviate the country's ills, especially since 1964, have scored some notable gains in solving our problem. This, the late President Lyndon Baines Johnson declared, is "to make the quality of American life — and I mean life for *all* Americans — match the quantity of our wealth."[2]

On the scoreboard of attainment toward this goal may be listed such accomplishments as civil rights acts that removed serious barriers to equality, federal aid and incentives toward improved education, legal enactments against pollution, and practical steps toward rebuilding our cities and eliminating hard-core poverty.

Will We Fail and the Dream Fade?

Despite these initial successes, new problems develop apparently as fast as older ones are promised solution. As a nation, we must begin to see that our basic difficulty has become moral and spiritual. Contempt for time-honored codes of conduct, with crime and lawlessness skyrocketing, are making a mirage of our "great society" and causing it to recede farther and farther into the ever-widening desert of our spiritual barrenness.

What a tragedy to have to discover by sad experience that our billion-dollar economy cannot buy us inner peace and security, or cure our national and international ills. When will we learn that in seeking a better social order, we dare not substitute gold for God? Only when we have learned this lesson will the unprecedented flow of legislative acts designed to bring in the great society bring us the realization of our dream. If we fail, the intolerable alternative may well prove to be a nightmare of distrust and dissension in a divided nation, split into hostile camps.

As America approaches her second centennial on July 4, 1976, she stands at the crossroads. Before her lies the road of faith in God and in one's fellowman under God. This is the road the nation has travelled for the first 200 years of her history. This course has brought her to a pinnacle of prosperity and power unparalleled among the nations of the earth. It has inspired her with an unshakable confidence that she has been specially blessed by Providence.

This same road of success, broader now and more expansive, leads on to new heights of greatness. But the question is, Will America continue on this route as she prepares to enter the third century of her national existence? Or will she take another road that leads downward from the heights — the road that abandons faith in God and that engenders distrust in one's fellowman?

The words of President Johnson, one of the most ardent advocates of the great society, are significant. "What happens to us will depend on what individual Americans resolve to do — or what they neglect and lose heart in doing."[3]

LIMITATIONS OF THE HUMAN DREAM

No matter what success may attend the efforts of men in America, or elsewhere, to attain a utopian political and social order, insofar as it is human, it will contain weaknesses and inequities. Consequently it will fall short of the divine ideal. The divine pattern, however, will be realized only as God intervenes and the kingdom of Christ is established on the earth.

A number of reasons are set forth in Scripture why the political and social utopias of men are fraught with serious imperfections. One of the most important is that the human race is fallen. Subject to a sinful nature, unredeemed men are prone to every sort of evil. Hatred, war, strife, lawlessness, immorality, and greed smolder like a seething volcano in the heart of fallen man. Even redeemed men, who are endowed with a new nature, must continually rely upon the indwelling Spirit to enable them to live in the power of the new life they receive from God (Gal 5:16-24).

In addition to the old Adamic nature, which may be considered as an enemy within, there are spiritual foes without. These seek to work through the enemy within. Satan and demon spirits operate through the old nature (Eph 6:10-12; Col 1:13). They incite men to rebel against God and to do every type of sin that mars men's laudable efforts on the political and social level.

Satan and demons operate not only through the old nature within the human personality, they also are active in the outside world. This evil world system is prominent in Scripture and constitutes the political and governmental sphere in which Satan is particularly active (Eph 6:12; 1 Jn 2:15-17).

Since every ideal society proposed by man must be set up in the satanic world system, it must at best be tarnished by the evil of this system. Such an order administered by men with a fallen nature (even regenerated men still possess an old unrenewed nature alongside the new nature), of necessity will be characterized by imperfection and inequity. Those who administer the order as well as those over whom they administer are both subject to weakness and limitation. The order itself must accordingly be subject to the same weakness and limitation.

Only as Satan and his hosts are bound in the abyss at the second advent of Christ (Rev 20:1-3) will the satanic system be destroyed. Only then can the truly great society be realized. And it will be God's, not man's. Christ will replace fallen, fallible men as kingdom Ruler. Christ's glorified and sin-freed saints will rule with Him.

It is true those over whom Christ and His glorified saints will rule will still be unglorified, and hence subject to the old sinful nature. But the vast majority of earth's population in that era will know and gladly serve the Lord. Sinners and evildoers, moreover, will be dealt with swiftly and severely (Ps 2:8-12; Rev 19:15).

The result will be a social order based on justice and righteousness. It will bring man the golden age for which he has longed and which the prophets of God have envisioned from dim antiquity.

At last the prayer our Lord taught His disciples will be realized.

"Our Father who art in heaven, Hallowed be Thy name. Thy kingdom come. Thy will be done, On earth as it is in heaven" (Mt 6:9-10, NASB).

Then, when heaven comes into closest communication with earth, will Jacob's glorious vision at Bethel (Gen 28:12) and the wonderful prophetic words spoken by our Lord to Nathaniel be fulfilled. "Truly, truly, I say to you, you shall see the heavens opened, and the angels of God ascending and descending upon the Son of Man" (Jn 1:51, NASB).

Coming — a Warless World

War among nations, tensions and hostilities among individuals constitute one of the greatest barriers to mankind in its relentless search for a perfect social order. How ironic that the twentieth century, which has witnessed mankind's greatest strides in science and technological advance and its greatest strivings for social justice, should witness two global wars of unparalleled magnitude, besides innumerable nonglobal conflicts.

Trying to stop a hot war, or attempting to keep a cold war from becoming a hot one, is the almost frenzied activity of a host of diplomats and emissaries of peace the world over. The old League of Nations became defunct. The present-day United Nations represents an international organization that is seeking to bring peace to a war-weary world.

Meanwhile, untold billions of dollars are being spent on military research and preparation. Among the superpowers, the race is to become so strong that no aggressor will attack, out of fear of retaliation. Meanwhile, the threat of nuclear annihilation hangs like a Damoclean sword over a distraught world, threatening man's great society with ruin.

In the face of this dark picture, the prophetic Word promises a social order free of war in a golden age of peace. God will accomplish this, not by bigger military budgets, greater armaments and armies, or peace organizations; He will send Christ, "the Prince of Peace." It is declared, "Of the increase of his government and peace there shall be no end, upon the throne of David, and upon his kingdom, to order it, and to establish it with justice and with righteousness from henceforth even forever" (Is 9:7, New Scofield).

Peace shall fill the earth, because righteousness will prevail everywhere as the result of Christ's rule. "And he shall judge among the nations, and shall rebuke many peoples; and they shall beat their swords into plowshares, and their spears into pruning hooks; nation shall not lift up sword against nation, neither shall they learn war any more" (Is 2:4, New Scofield).

Then the United States Military Academy at West Point, the United States Naval Academy at Annapolis, and the Air Force Academy at Colorado Springs, as well as the military, naval, and air-force academies of the other nations, will no longer exist. The reason is simple: they will not be needed any longer. Mankind will no longer make preparing for war and waging war a science, as is the case today.

Christ will speak peace to the nations, and universal peace will fill the millennial earth.

Imagine a Society Without Crime

Lawlessness and crime vie with war as the chief impediment in the way of man's realizing a utopian society. Widespread abandonment of divine standards of morality has produced contempt for the law and law enforcement agencies. Coupled with this is a lack of speedy trials and significant punishment. The result is an astronomical rise in the crime rate and the cost of trying to control lawlessness.

The headline of the *Baltimore Evening Sun,* dated August 16, 1972, is typical and tells the story of violence abroad in the land. "Two Murdered on City Streets; Homicide Toll at 200 for Year. Number Is 18 Ahead of '71 Record Total."

The first reaction of the government is to attempt to curb the evil rather than to get at the real cause and effect a cure. Billions are appropriated to study ways and means of controlling the runaway situation. But how futile to seek to deal effectively with a problem that is basically internal in a purely external way. Lawlessness is but the outward manifestation of an inward rebellion against God and the eternal moral code He has established for all human beings.

Scripture predicts the establishment of a society where crime will be nonexistent. The problem of lawlessness will be solved. This will come about, however, not by man's way, with huge expenditures for crime research and the increase of law-enforcing agencies; God's way will be to deal with both the cause and the cure of lawlessness.

Regarding His people Israel in the new social order He will establish, God declares, "I will put my law in their inward parts, and write it in their hearts; and will be their God, and they shall be my people" (Jer 31:33). Keeping God's law will be spontaneous for Israelites. "For they shall all know me, from the least of them unto the greatest of them, saith the LORD" (Jer 31:34).

Gentiles shall learn God's laws from converted Israel and submit to God's ways as a result. "And many nations shall come, and say, Come, and let us go up to the mountain of the LORD, and to the house of the God of Jacob; and he will teach us of his ways, and we will walk in his paths (Mic 4:2).

But the Lord will deal with wrongdoing not only internally but also externally, if the need arises. He will summarily and severely punish those who attempt to practice lawlessness. "Thou shalt break them with a rod of iron; Thou shalt dash them in pieces like a potter's jar. Now therefore, O kings, act wisely; be warned, O rulers of the earth. Serve the LORD reverently and rejoice with trembling. Kiss the Son, lest He be angry and you perish in the way; for soon shall His wrath be kindled" (Ps 2:9-12, Berkeley).

All this means that God's great society will solve the problem of crime. The reigning King of kings and Lord of lords will not only strike down the wicked with the rod of His mouth and root out rebels at the beginning of His reign, He will transform men's hearts so that they will spontaneously walk in His ways. Those born during the kingdom age who refuse to own Christ as Saviour and remain unregenerate will be compelled to restrain any criminal manifestations in conduct. Christ and His coadministrators, the glorified saints, will bring swift and irremediable punishment upon evildoers, so that all evildoing will be brought to a sudden end.

FAREWELL TO IGNORANCE

Next to war and crime, ignorance is perhaps the greatest obstacle to man's realizing a utopian order on the earth. The irony of the situation is that ignorance abounds in the midst of the most advanced age of science and enlightenment the world has ever known. Daniel foresaw it as "the time of the end" when "knowledge shall be increased" (Dan 12:4).

While it is true multiplied millions in many underprivileged nations of the world are still illiterate, ignorance is still a problem among the most literate peoples of the world. This is the case because much of our knowledge is divorced from God and is powerless to transform life and character. Our civilized learning ignores the basic truth that true education and true knowledge have their beginning in "the fear of the LORD" (Pr 1:7).

Today we take the Word of God, prayer, and the inculcation of sound morality out of our educational systems. In doing so, we do not seem to realize that we have left only a foundation of sand upon which to build the type of citizenship that has made this nation great and that alone will perpetuate its greatness. We speak of "quality education" and seem to think that merely pouring billions of dollars into educational institutions will achieve it. Strangely enough, we leave out the chief ingredient of "quality education," which is the knowledge of the Lord.

The coming golden age our Lord will inaugurate at His second advent will be possible because "the knowledge of the LORD" will fill men's hearts and lives "as the waters cover the sea" (Is 11:9).

In that ideal society, true life-transforming knowledge will produce sterling character. "They shall teach no more every man his neighbour, and every man his brother, saying, Know the LORD: for they shall all know me, from the least of them unto the greatest of them" (Jer 31:34).

Knowing the Lord, men will love Him and love one another. As the apostle John declares, "The one who does not love does not know God, for God is love" (1 Jn 4:8, NASB). An ideal social order must be founded on love. That love comes from knowing God. That is why the ultimate great society must be God's, not man's.

ONE DAY JUSTICE WILL PREVAIL

Another great hindrance to man's attainment of his utopian social dreams is the problem of injustice. The removal of inequities because of race, color, and creed, has been a long, uphill struggle, consuming many centuries.

In this area, man has made significant strides. But it took almost a century after the Civil War and the abolition of slavery in America for significant progress in civil rights to be made. Many inequities in this and other areas still exist. Even the progress two centuries of struggle in America have accomplished may well be lost. This tragedy can easily happen, unless we carefully guard the foundation of our liberties.

The forces of tyranny at work in worldwide Communism, which has engulfed huge segments of earth's population, offer a real threat to the free world. Man's struggle for justice, liberty, and humanity is being dealt a serious setback by this sinister form of social slavery.

Only by the advent of Christ's kingdom will injustice and every type of oppression be abolished. Only then will the perfect social order be established that men are so vainly trying to introduce through their own ideas and efforts.

Isaiah foresaw Christ in the coming kingdom, administering justice to the Gentiles, who were the despised and downtrodden of the prophet's times. "Behold my servant, whom I uphold; mine elect, in whom my soul delighteth; I have put my Spirit upon him; he shall bring forth justice to the nations" (Is 42:1, New Scofield).

The prophet further declares that Messiah "shall not fail nor be discouraged, till he have set justice in the earth; and the coasts shall wait for his law" (Is 42:4, New Scofield).

No More Poverty and Hunger

Destitution, malnutrition, and even starvation have been the lot of millions of impoverished people throughout the world from time immemorial. The twentieth century with its scientific progress and know-how is no exception. Famines in India, China, and other parts of the world in recent times have taken a great toll in human life. The present-day population explosion haunts scientists with the specter of insufficient food to feed earth's population, rapidly pushing toward the six billion mark.

Even in the United States, where food is produced in huge quantities, there are people who are underfed and undernourished, particularly among the mountain poor of Appalachia and the rural poor of the South.

Hunger, U.S.A., a report by the Citizens' Board of Inquiry into Hunger and Malnutrition in the United States, estimated that from ten to fourteen and a half million Americans may be endangered by anemia, mental retardation, secondary infection, or premature death because of a deficient diet.[4] Meanwhile, Congress and the U.S. department of agriculture have spent billions to stop the overproduction of food, but only a fraction as much to ease the pains of undereating.

All who have attempted to plan a better society for man upon this earth have had to struggle relentlessly, often unsuccessfully, with the problem of hunger and poverty. Christ's millennial kingdom is envisioned as a time of unparalleled material bounty, when *all* mankind's needs will be met "in the face of spiraling population explosion."[5]

Isaiah predicts that "the wilderness and the dry land shall be glad; the desert shall rejoice and blossom as the rose. It shall blossom abundantly and rejoice with delight and singing" (Is 35:1-2, Berkeley).

Amos rejoices in the prospect of the day when "the plowman shall overtake the reaper, and the treader of grapes him who scatters the seed. The mountains shall drip new wine, and all the hills shall dissolve" (Amos 9:13).

There will no longer exist "the have" and "the have-not" nations. All nations and all peoples will have in abundance. Destitution and malnutrition will be unknown. Poverty will be a thing of the past.

REMOVING THE PERILS OF PROSPERITY

A great society cannot exist where wealth fails to enrich all citizens of a commonwealth. The United States, for instance, has been favored with an unprecedented growth in economy. From the Civil War period until 1900, its progress spread like a prairie fire. Since 1900 it has mushroomed like an explosion. During the four years of World War II, the American economy doubled. In the quarter of a century that followed, we built on top of that economy another twice as big again.

This fantastic prosperity has produced problems of inner-city poverty and squalor, pollution of air and waterways, and gaping inequities among our people. An estimated twenty-two million poor Americans exist in the squalid shadows of our immense wealth.

To combat this situation, anti-poverty programs, capital-labor arbitration, and minimum wage laws have sought to distribute our enormous gross income. Antipollution regulations and plans for rehabilitation of inner city slums and other projects only help to keep the problem under some control, but offer no complete solution.

In Christ's ideal kingdom, however, there is promised prosperity and blessing for all. Christ Himself will prohibit any amassing of wealth that is selfish or that hurts others or harms the physical environment. He promises, "They shall not hurt nor destroy in all my holy mountain" (Is 11:9).

DIVINE HEALING AND MEDICARE

The problem of disease and sickness has always baffled the planners of a better society. Although great strides have been made in medical research, health insurance, and Medicare programs, skyrocketing hospital and medical costs have undermined the security of many sick and aged people in present-day society.

God's answer to this problem will be different from man's.

Christ Himself will intervene in curing illness and disease. Even the crippled and hopelessly incapacitated person will be restored to normal health.

"No resident there will say, 'I am sick,' for the people living there will have had their sins forgiven" (Is 33:24, Berkeley). "For I will restore health to you, and I will heal your wounds, says the LORD, because they have called you an outcast, 'It is Zion, for whom no one cares!'" (Jer 30:17, Berkeley).

Isaiah comments on the miraculous cures that will take place in Christ's earthly kingdom. "Then shall the eyes of the blind be opened, and the ears of the deaf unstopped. Then shall the lame man leap like a deer, and the tongue of the dumb shall sing, because waters shall break forth in the wilderness and streams in the desert" (Is 35:5-6, Berkeley).

These mighty healings will be a manifestation of "the powers of the age to come" (Heb 6:5, NASB).

THE SACRED SUPPLANTS THE SECULAR

Perhaps the most important single factor that has marked man's greatest efforts for a better social order with a large degree of futility is the growing spirit of secularism of our day. Men imagine that God can be removed from our daily life and mankind can be prosperous and happy. The phenomenal rise of Communism offers a glaring example. But godlessness is not confined to the countries enslaved behind the iron and bamboo curtains.

The Western or free world, which has had a predominantly Christian heritage, is being victimized by a colossal and terrifying secularistic trend that is coldly and calculatingly attempting to remove God and Christian morality from every phase of our daily living. This increased secularization of our society is the root of our present-day troubles. These crowd in upon us despite our best human efforts to solve them by our own wisdom and huge expenditures of money. We seem oblivious to the fact that a godless society cannot be a law-abiding society or long remain a free society, or be a really happy or prosperous society.

What is worse, we fail to see that secular education and human government cannot do what only God can do — change a sinner's heart. Only God can instill in men's hearts His love, causing them to love Him and one another and to keep His moral laws. This Christ will do when He returns to set up His perfect social order.

Then the secular shall be banished. Every phase of life will be sacred in God's great society. Zechariah enunciates this great truth in a graphic way in a classic passage: "In that day there shall be inscribed on the bells of the horses, 'HOLY TO THE LORD.' Even the pots in the house of the LORD, as well as the bowls before the altar, every pot in Jerusalem and Judah shall be holy to the LORD of hosts" (Zec 14:20-21, Berkeley).

Such mundane things as the jingling bells on a horse's bridle shall attest the Lord's holiness. The most common kitchen utensil shall be as holy as the sacred vessels of the temple. Why? Because God's perfect social order will have been established. In this kingdom, everything and everyone will be dedicated to the great King and Lord, the mighty Christ — Creator-Redeemer, Healer, and Provider. Gladly and spontaneously everyone will worship, love, serve, and obey Him.

He alone will bring in the kingdom of righteousness and peace. He alone will cause mankind's dream of a golden age to come true. He created and redeemed man. Only He can fully satisfy man and provide him the perfect social order he has longed for through the ages.

13

Hell and the Fate of the Wicked

ONE OF THE MOST SATISFYING ASPECTS of the prophetic Word is its full disclosure of the future of all created beings. This revelation includes the destiny of the good and evil angels as well as the saved and unsaved of the human race. No angel or human being need be in darkness or doubt concerning what lies ahead for him. God has plainly written it out, so that all may take heed, be forewarned, and act accordingly.

In the case of angelic beings, their destiny is fixed and unalterable. The elect, unfallen angels are confirmed in goodness and will inhabit heaven, the new Jerusalem, and a sin-cleansed universe with the saved of the human family. On the other hand, the fallen, wicked angels, including Satan, are confirmed in rebellion. They, with the unsaved of the human family, will be consigned eternally to Gehenna, which is eternal hell.[1]

Fallen mankind is offered salvation through the death and resurrection of Jesus Christ, incarnate Deity, the God-Man, and Redeemer. Those who believe on Jesus Christ's redemptive atonement for sin, receive eternal life and in eternity will inhabit heaven and the New Jerusalem in a sin-cleansed universe. Those who reject Christ's saving work must share the fate of Satan and fallen angels in Gehenna for eternity (Mt 25:41; Rev 20:14-15).

SATAN'S BINDING IN THE ABYSS

When Christ returns to earth, Satan, the prime instigator of earth's evils and man's woes, must be dealt with before Christ's kingdom can be established on this globe. Hence, in the book of the Revelation, the vision of Christ's return is followed immediately by that of Satan's being confined to the abyss during the kingdom age.

The abyss is the prison of the demons. When the demons were expelled from the demoniac of Gadara, they begged our Lord not to send them into the abyss (Lk 8:31). They preferred to enter swine, evidently in order to remain among the free demons. They caused the death of the swine, so that they might again be free to indwell men. Spirits that are now in the abyss are the imprisoned demons. Multitudes of these will be released as part of the tribulation judgments to torment wicked earth dwellers (Rev 9:1-12).

John the apostle "saw an angel coming down from heaven, having the key of the abyss and a great chain in his hand. And he laid hold of the dragon, the serpent of old, who is the Devil and Satan, and bound him for a thousand years, and threw him into the abyss, and shut it and sealed it over him, so that he should not deceive the nations any longer, until the thousand years were completed" (Rev 20:1-3, NASB).

This prophetic scene not only signifies Satan's incarceration in the prison of the demons, but the confining of the demons also, both those who are now free and those let loose during the tribulation. That the demons will also share in Satan's imprisonment is revealed by the prophet Zechariah. "And it shall come to pass in that day, saith the LORD of hosts, that I will cut off the names of the idols . . . and also I will cause the prophets and the unclean spirit to pass out of the land" (Zec 13:2).

"The unclean spirit" (literally, spirit of uncleanness) is a collective designation standing for "spirits of uncleanness" or demon-energizers of idolatry and false prophetism rampant in the earth at the time of Christ's advent.[2]

The binding of both Satan and his demon aids is necessary, because the kingdom has for its object the restoration of the divine authority in the earth. Opposing this is not only Satan as the chief antagonist but his demon assistants who are one with him in his rebellion against God.

The Doom of the Beast and the False Prophet

While Satan and his demon hordes are remanded to the abyss, his chief tools on earth are visited with swift judgment. "And the beast was seized, and with him the false prophet who performed the signs in his presence, by which he deceived those who had received the mark of the beast and those who worshiped his image; these two were thrown alive into the lake of fire which burns with brimstone" (Rev 19:20, NASB).

The beast is the Antichrist, head of the Roman empire revived, the confederated states of Europe of the end time (Rev 13:1-10). As Christ is God incarnate, so the beast (Antichrist) apparently will be Satan incarnate. Evidently he will be begotten in the womb of a woman by the power of Satan as Christ was conceived in the virgin's womb by the Holy Spirit. He will be the devil-man as Christ is the God-Man.

Earth dwellers will then worship "the dragon, because he gave his authority to the beast." They will also "worship the beast" as the manifestation of Satan in human form (Rev 13:4, NASB).

It is at this point that mystical Babylon, discussed in chapter 3, will come into being, with Satan as its founder. Satan's imitation of the triune God will then be attempted. The Dragon (Satan) corresponds to God the Father. The Antichrist (beast) corresponds to God the Son. The false prophet corresponds to God the Holy Spirit (cf. Rev 16:13).

As the devil-man, the Antichrist (beast) accordingly will be a real man, but more than a man. In a sense he will be a "superman," one with Satan as his father, as our Lord was one with God His Father (Jn 10:30).

The false prophet will also be a man but more than a man — not in the sense of being unable to die physically, as Norman B. Harrison holds,[3] nor in the sense of Satan-begotten, as the Antichrist is. The false prophet is also a superman, evidently in the sense of being so filled with the spirit of Satan and demonic power that he will be a resistless deceiver and miracle-worker.

These two, instead of being killed physically, as the demon-driven armies at Armageddon, are taken "alive" and thrown into Gehenna (eternal hell) at once. Eternal judgment is not delayed, as in the case of *all* other unregenerate men; but because of the enormity of their crime, the Antichrist and the false prophet are punished immediately. Other sinners eventually go to Gehenna through physical death via intermediate hell (hades). These two are hurled immediately into the place of eternal punishment.

As W. Kelly observes, "They were caught in flagrant treason and rebellion against Jehovah and His Christ. What further need of any process of judgment?"[4]

In contrast to the special fate of the beast and the false prophet, "The rest were killed with the sword which came from the mouth of him who sat upon the horse, and all the birds were filled with their flesh" (Rev 19:21, NASB). Their doom of physical death was just. But by no means was it as decisively severe as that of the two leaders of the end-time rebellion.

THE RESURRECTION BODY OF THE UNSAVED

The beast and the false prophet are sentenced to eternal death without experiencing physical death. This apparently means they receive at once the kind of a body *all* unregenerate humanity will receive at the second resurrection to condemnation, when the unsaved are cast into Gehenna after the great white throne judgment (Rev 20:14-15).

What this resurrection body of the unsaved is like, is not revealed in Scripture. But just as Enoch and Elijah in the Old Testament were translated to heaven without dying, and the church saints of the New Testament living at the time of the rapture will receive a glorified body apart from the experience of physical death, so there will be two unsaved persons who will not die physically. Because of their special wickedness, they will be exceptions to the universal law of physical death for unregenerate humanity. "It is appointed for men to die once, and after this comes judgment" (Heb 9:27, NASB). Their judgment will merit the second death, the lake of fire (Rev 20:14). It will be swift, irremediable, and apart from physical death.

Evidently the physical, mortal frame of the beast and that of the false prophet will be instantly changed into bodies still human but indestructible and fitted to suffer eternally in the spiritual realm, denoted symbolically by the figure of the "lake of fire which burns with brimstone" (Rev 19:20, NASB).

That the resurrected body of the unsaved is indestructible is proved by the fact that these two foes of God, whose bodies are changed apart from physical death, to receive the kind of body all unsaved people will get in the second resurrection, are still suffering the vengeance of eternal fire a thousand years after they were cast into Gehenna (Rev 20:10).

Hence, it is clear that annihilation of the wicked is not a scriptural doctrine. It is not to be predicated of the body and certainly not of the soul and spirit of man.

Moreover, the resurrection body of the unsaved will be eternal and indestructible, like the resurrection body of the saved. But in contrast to the resurrected body of the redeemed, it will of course not be sinless, painless, nor deathless, since it will be subject to eternal death in the sense of being everlastingly cut off and separated from God in conscious torment in Gehenna (Rev 20:14-15).

The Intermediate State of the Unsaved

The beast and the false prophet, in being cast *alive* into Gehenna, as noted above, offer an exception to the normal fate of the unsaved, who at death go to hades, *not* Gehenna. The armies at Armageddon, put to death by the returning Christ (Rev 19:21), furnish an illustration of this, as do *all* the unsaved from Adam to the end of time.

Our Lord, in the story of the rich man and Lazarus (Lk 16:19-31), lifts the curtain of life after death, revealing the place of departed souls, both saved and unsaved, between death and the resurrection.

Hell (hades, Greek, and sheol, Hebrew) is the place *all* the dead apparently went in Old Testament times (Lk 16:23). The righteous went to "Abraham's bosom" (Lk 16:22), but were separated from the wicked Old Testament dead by a "great gulf" (Lk 16:26).

The repentant thief on the cross next to Christ (Lk 23:43) went to be with Christ that day "in paradise." Apparently, in the light of Ephesians 4:8-10, paradise, or Abraham's bosom, since Christ's ascension, has been transferred to "the third heaven" (2 Co 12:1-4), the immediate presence of God (1 Co 15:53; 2 Co 5:2, 4; Phil 1:23; 1 Th 4:13-18).

The *unsaved* of both the Old and New Testament periods, however, still go to hades (intermediate hell). They are there in a discarnate state (soul and spirit separated from the body) but in conscious torment (Lk 16:24).

At the sinners' judgment before the great white throne (Rev 20:11-15), the wicked are resurrected. Soul and spirit are reunited to a changed body adapted to the spiritual and eternal realm. In the body reunited to soul and spirit, the wicked are judged and cast into eternal hell, together with death and hades (Rev 20:4). This is called in Scripture the "second death" because it involves separation from God in Gehenna, "the lake of fire," for all eternity (Rev 20:14). It is the final state of the unsaved.

Satan's Final Doom

As noted above, Satan and his demons are imprisoned in the abyss during the millennium (Zec 13:2; Rev 20:1-3). After his thousand-year imprisonment, Satan is set free from the abyss. The purpose of his loosing, in God's program, is that the archrebel might test man's loyalty to God under the ideal conditions of the kingdom as the last of God's ordered ages in time, before the dawn of eternity.

Satan's success in stirring up a worldwide rebellion (Rev 20:7-9) furnishes ample proof that the heart of fallen man is "deceitful above all things, and desperately wicked" (Jer 17:9) and that even regenerated but unglorified humanity, because of the presence of the old Adamic nature, is also capable of great evil.

The rebels in Satan's final uprising will evidently be individuals among the kingdom nations who yielded only feigned allegiance to Messiah's stringent rule of iron (Ps 2:9; 18:44; 66:3; 81:15). The revolt will be completely crushed by divine omnipotence.

The destruction of the rebels will mark the end of God's toleration of evil upon the earth. The demonstration God intends for all the universe will be accomplished. He will show that fallen man, even under the ideal conditions of a golden age, presided over by Christ Himself, is inveterately wicked.

The Creator will prove to all created beings that Christ's redemption on the cross, guaranteeing man a glorified body, is the only way a sin-cleansed universe will be realized. He will illustrate to every creature that Gehenna, the one isolation ward for sinners, is an absolute necessity. If such a sinless order is to be brought in and perpetuated, all sinners, both angelic and human, must be rigidly confined and never again permitted to introduce sin and rebellion into God's creation.

Men in every age have derided and scoffed at the idea of hell and the eternal punishment of the wicked. God will once and for all silence every tongue and still all criticism, as He quells Satan's last rebellion and casts the devil into Gehenna.

The divine account of the destruction of the last of earth's rebels is terse and terrible. "And fire came down from heaven and devoured them. And the devil who deceived them was thrown into the lake of fire and brimstone, where the beast and the false prophet are also; and they shall be tormented day and night forever and ever" (Rev 20:9-10, NASB).

The fact that the beast and the false prophet are still alive and conscious in Gehenna when Satan is cast into the same place one thousand years later is significant. It proves, as H. A. Ironside so aptly says, "that the lake of fire is not annihilation and that it is not purgatorial either, for it neither annihilates nor purifies these two fallen foes of God and man after a thousand years under judgment."[5]

Satan's predestined judgment is at last executed. The vital head wound suffered in prophesied encounter with the virgin-born seed of the woman (Gen 3:15) now proves fatal. First cast out of the heavenly realms onto the earth (Rev 12:9), then imprisoned in the abyss (Rev 20:1-3), the devil is now consigned to his eternal fate in the lake of fire prepared for him and his evil angels (Mt 25:41). "Fire and brimstone" speak symbolically of unimaginable torment

(Rev 14:10) in the spirit world, *not* the natural world. The phrase "forever and ever" means eternally, everlastingly.

The punishment of the wicked in Gehenna is as eternal as God's throne, for both are said to be "forever and ever" (Rev 20:10; cf. Heb 1:8).

The Resurrection of the Unsaved

The "second resurrection," to condemnation and eternal death, is distinct from the "first resurrection," which is to glorification and eternal life (Lk 14:14). The precise interval between these two separate resurrections is revealed to be the thousand years of the kingdom age (Rev 20:5).

Those who are raised in the second resurrection are all the unregenerate from Eden to the end of the millennium. They comprise all the unsaved of all the ages of time. They are resurrected so that soul and spirit in hades might be reunited to the body fitted for the spiritual realm.

This second resurrection of the unsaved will evidently comprise the vast majority of the human race. Hence, the divine throne before which they are resurrected to stand is said to be "great," since it must accommodate billions upon billions of the lost (Rev 20:11).

John the apostle glimpsed the magnitude of the scene. "And I saw the dead, the great and the small, standing before the throne . . . And the sea gave up the dead which were in it, and death and Hades gave up the dead which were in them" (Rev 20:12-13, NASB).

The Judgment of the Unsaved

The scene of judgment closes the kingdom, the last of God's ordered ages in time, and marks the dawn of eternity. "Earth and heaven" are said to flee away before the throne-sitter and Judge, to make way for "a new heaven and a new earth" of the sin-cleansed eternity that follows (Rev 20:11; 21:1).

Since the scene concerns the unsaved dead resurrected to be judged, they are envisioned as standing before "a great white throne." It is "white" because it represents divine righteousness and purity, which characterize God and His absolutely just decisions.

The Judge who sits upon the throne is Christ, to whom the Father has "given all judgment" (Jn 5:22, NASB). He has already judged "the living" (cf. Mt 25:31); now the mighty throne-sitter is about to judge "the dead" (2 Ti 4:1, NASB).

The vast multitudes of the unsaved stand in shame and agony before the infinite holiness of God, uncovered and unprotected by the blood of Christ. Since the multitude represents the lost, the issue to be adjudicated is not salvation, but works. They are judged as unsaved persons according to their response to the eternal moral law of God and the resulting *quality of their life* as unregenerate human beings.

Lest this important point involving the purpose of the judgment should be missed, it is purposely emphasized by repetition. "And the dead were judged from the things which were written in the books, according to their deeds. And the sea gave up the dead which were in it, and death and Hades gave up the dead which were in them; and they were judged, every one of them according to their deeds" (Rev 20:12*b*-13, NASB).

GOD'S MORAL LAW AND THE SINNERS' JUDGMENT

Often an important truth is lost sight of, and that is that *all* men, whether regenerate or unregenerate, will be judged before God according to their deeds in this life. The regenerate are saved solely by faith in divine, redemptive grace, manifested in Christ (Eph 2:8-10). However, they are responsible to live a godly, useful life of service, for they will be rewarded or suffer loss of reward at the judgment seat of Christ for their response to God's eternal moral law (2 Co 5:10), as has been pointed out in chapter 5.

God's eternal moral law is reflected in the Mosaic Decalogue (Ex 20:1-17). But it is as eternal as God is, and the Creator requires it of *all* His creatures. Keeping God's law cannot save the unsaved or keep the saved saved. Keeping it, however, by cooperation with the indwelling Spirit, can produce a high quality of life in the believer, producing Spirit-indited works. These will be rewarded at the believer's judgment.⁶

The unregenerate will also be judged by the same moral laws. "But," it may be asked, "how can God righteously judge the unsaved according to His moral laws when they are unable to keep them?" The answer is, "They are, as helpless sinners of Adam's fallen race, unable to keep God's moral laws to merit salvation from God. But they are *not* unable to keep the moral laws of God, outwardly and to a degree, to live decent, respectable, law-abiding lives, even though unsaved."

It is obvious from common observation that unsaved people vary as much in their quality of life as saved people do. There is the temperate, charitable, unsaved person and the intemperate, uncharitable, saved person. There is the carnal, loose-living believer and the well-disciplined, morally tempered, unsaved religionist.

Although an infinitely just, loving, and righteous God can never permit any unsaved person, no matter how good in himself, or moral or religious, to go to heaven, he *must* deal with such a person on the basis of what he has done on earth. Only in this manner could God judge impartially and righteously.

Many heathen may never have had a chance to hear the gospel and accept Christ. But they had the witness of God's glory and deity written in nature (Ps 19:1-5; Ro 1:19-20). Moreover, as creatures of God, they had God's moral law written in their conscience, so that they are without excuse to live up to the light they had. They will be judged according to that light and their response to it, in the kind of a life they lived.

This is precisely the reason why God must judge all men according to their works. Believers and unbelievers must realize they are held accountable for what they do. Let this truth deter wicked men from their wicked deeds. They will answer for them. Let this fact guard any sinner from saying, "Since I reject Christ and choose hell, I might as well live lawlessly and recklessly." Such folly forgets that "going to heaven" is not a matter of sinning or not sinning, but in trusting Christ for one's sin. This argument also forgets that sinners who go to hell will be judged for their works, as well as saints that go to heaven.

This truth behooves all men, saved as well as unsaved, to live the best possible life, by observing the commandments of God. These are the basis and the norm of all right living, and the foundation of our civil laws and law-enforcing agencies. Let sinners be assured, if they escape punishment at the hands of human judges, they will not do so before the all-seeing Judge at the great white throne, before whose infinitely holy face heaven and earth will flee away.

Degrees of Punishment of the Unsaved

As the saved differ in their response to the moral law of God, and hence in their reward in heaven, the unsaved differ also in their response to the divine commands, and hence in their punishment in hell. This simply means there will be degrees of reward for the righteous in heaven and degrees of punishment for the unrighteous in hell.

What eternal hell or Gehenna is like is not specifically spelled out, except that it will be a place and a condition of eternal torment. But certainly the torment will not be the same for all the unsaved. Many in hell will be religious, moral, law-abiding people, like many unsaved church members in America, or like self-disciplined Buddhists or Confucianists in non-Christian religions.

Such "good" unsaved people will be beaten with "few stripes" (Lk 12:47-48). Other "bad" unsaved people, who have broken every law of God and man, will be beaten with "many stripes." This is the obvious connotation of all sinners being judged "according to their deed" or "works" (Rev 20:12-13). It is, moreover, the necessary corollary of an infinitely just, loving, and righteous Judge. He will accord each denizen the place and the punishment in Gehenna his life on earth has merited in His omniscient eyes.

The Judgment of Millennial Saints

While the great white throne judgment is predominantly the judgment of the unsaved, it is of necessity not exclusively so. It must also include saints who have lived and died during the kingdom age. Although longevity will be restored during this period, yet both the saved and the unsaved people of that period will die. These must be resurrected before the eternal state.

It is a recognized fact that the unsaved of the millennium will come up with the rest of the dead of all preceding ages. But what is not generally recognized is that the saved of this period, who have died, must be resurrected and appear at this inquest. The unsaved living at the conclusion will join Satan's final revolt and be put to death. The saved then living will probably be translated and judged at the same judgment. It thus appears that the tail end of the first resurrection to life will be coterminous with the second resurrection to condemnation. This is what the apostle Paul meant when he described the various stages of the first resurrection (1 Co 15:20-23). Then, he declares, comes "the end" (1 Co 15:24), by which he means the end of the first resurrection at the end of the millennium, when Christ delivers the kingdom to God the Father and the eternal state is initiated.

The point is that there will be saved resurrected, who have died during the kingdom, and saved translated at the end of it, who must appear for adjudication of their works at the same time as the unsaved at the great white throne. This is why "the book of life" appears alongside of the "books" that record the deeds of the unsaved (Rev 20:12).

The "book of life" will doubtlessly serve a double purpose. It will contain the names of the saved of the kingdom age and a record of their works. It will also furnish evidence to every unsaved person that he was really lost with no claim upon eternal life in Christ. Undoubtedly a lot of "good," moral people will contest the divine sentence of their lost condition. The "book of life" will be decisive evidence against them, as it will not contain their name.

The issue will be transparently clear. "And if anyone's name was not found written in the book of life, he was thrown into the lake of fire" (Rev 20:15, NASB).

DEATH AND HADES CAST INTO GEHENNA

"And death and Hades were thrown into the lake of fire" (Rev 20:14, NASB). This is a necessary prelude to a sinless universe that will be realized in the eternal state. "The last enemy that will be abolished is death" (1 Co 15:26, NASB). This will not occur till after the kingdom age, when God becomes "all in all" in eternity. With all sin and sinners confined to Gehenna, death will never more occur in a perfected universe. Threefold life, spiritual, physical, and eternal, will never be tarnished by threefold death, spiritual, physical, and eternal, introduced into the human race by Satan at the fall.

But since physical death will never again occur in a sinless universe, it will be cast into Gehenna. There it will be swallowed up in eternal death, for the unsaved, who suffer the second death, will never again experience physical death and entrance into Sheol.

The destruction of death and hades in Gehenna signifies the perfect, sinless order God has planned for the eternal state. Gehenna will contain and confine all that would mar that glorious order God has been moving through the ages to bring to realization. Excluded from the splendors God is preparing for those who love Him "are the cowardly and unbelieving and abominable and murderers and immoral persons and sorcerers and idolaters, and all liars" (Rev 21:8, NASB).

GEHENNA IN GOD'S ETERNAL PURPOSE

Like everything in the divine economy, Gehenna has a purpose — a twofold purpose — one from the standpoint of the creature, the other from the standpoint of the Creator.

From the standpoint of the creature, "the lake of fire" will be a perpetual reminder of the folly of sin. It will flash like a danger signal, advertising to the universe of created beings, both angels and men, the utter futility of resisting God's will. It will act as an eternally potent deterrent to keep all created intelligences from the folly of Satan, demons, and wicked men.

The picture of Satan and the fallen angels and the plight of mankind deceived by him will be a grim reminder of the irretrievable ruin of sin.

From the standpoint of the Creator, the "lake of fire" will attest the glory and perfection of God. All else in a sin-cleansed universe of holy angels and glorified men will advertise the love, grace, majesty, and holiness of God. Gehenna will show His righteousness and justice as well. It will reveal how He dealt with sin and rebellion in unapproachable wisdom and infinite patience and holiness.

The incarceration of all practicers of evil in that dreadful abode will be an eternal witness to the power and severity (justice) of God, with even Satan's knee bowing, "even his tongue joining in the universal confession that Jesus Christ is Lord, to the glory of God the Father."[7]

14

Heaven and the Destiny
of the Redeemed

THE PROPHETIC WORD, in opening up one grand vista after another of God's plans and purposes for the future, reserves the most glorious for the last. As the telescope of prophecy pierces the curtain of time, it comes to focus upon eternity. Presented to our amazed gaze is a scene of such transcendent splendor that the human mind can scarcely take it in.

Sin has been dealt with, and all sinners, both angelic and human, consigned to one place and one abode. All the rest of the universe glows with the splendor of God's revealed glory and with the ecstatic joy and fellowship of sinless angels and redeemed glorified men.

The goal of all prophetic revelation has been reached. The voice of Him who is the Alpha and the Omega, the beginning and the end, utters a climactic declaration: "Behold, I am making all things new" (Rev 21:5, NASB). Through the prophetic telescope, we glimpse a new heaven and earth (Rev 21:1), a new fellowship (Rev 21:27), a new light (Rev 21:23-25), and a new paradise (Rev 22:1-5).

THE NEW HEAVEN AND THE NEW EARTH

The first amazing disclosure made concerning the sinless eternal state is that it will be ushered in by "a new heaven and a new earth; for the first heaven and the first earth passed away" (Rev 21:1, NASB). The obvious reference is to the declaration made that the first heaven and the first earth "fled away" (Rev 20:11) from the face of the Judge seated upon the great white throne.

"The first heaven and the first earth" is that part of creation ruined by sin (Gen 1:1-2). It is doomed to dissolution, not annihilation. The dissolution is effected by the fire of atomic fission. Peter describes this drastic renovation to make way for the conditions that shall prevail in eternity. He says, "The heavens will pass away with a roar and the elements will be destroyed with intense heat, and the earth and its works will be burned up." "But," the apostle continues, "according to His promise we are looking for new heavens and a new earth, in which righteousness dwells" (2 Pe 3:10, 13, NASB). The prophet Isaiah records the divine promise of a new heaven and a new earth in the Old Testament (Is 65:17; 66:22).

"Our planet," as Walter Scott aptly observes, "will be put in the crucible, altered, changed, and made new, to abide forever."[1]

The new earth, being eternal, will be adapted to the vast moral and physical changes which the eternal state necessitates. It is evidently to be the abode of the New Jerusalem and the habitation of saved and resurrected Israelites both of the Old Testament, tribulation, and millennial periods, as well as the saved nations (non-Israelites) of the kingdom age. The earthly millennial kingdom will merge into an eternal kingdom on the new earth.

The new heavens, as well as the New Jerusalem on the new earth, will be for the glorified saints of the church age. Accordingly, even in eternity, the abiding distinction will be preserved between the heavenly and earthly people of God. Thus the apostle speaks of "every family in heaven and on earth" (Eph 3:15, NASB).

STATE OF ABSOLUTE PERFECTION

Everything is new in the eternal state. Everything is according to God's glorious nature. The "new heavens" and "the new earth," the respective spheres of all the saved, shall be brought into blessed conformity with all that God is, in a state of fixed bliss and absolute perfection. The mediatorial kingdom of righteousness merges into the eternal perfect kingdom where God is "all in all" (1 Co 15:24-28).

In the mediatorial kingdom, righteousness reigned in the Person of the Messiah-King. Now it dwells. "It settles down, is at home, has come to stay."² Neither enemy nor evil shall ever again invade the spheres where the sinless angels and the glorified redeemed will dwell forever. From one end of a sin-cleansed universe to the other will reecho the joyous praises of creatures who love and worship the Creator and bask in His light and love.

No More Sea

The new earth of the eternal state evidences its completely renovated condition by a very significant detail the apocalyptic seer mentions: "And there is no longer any sea" (Rev 21:1, NASB).

The sea, which now constitutes over three-fifths of the earth's surface and which is absolutely essential to sustain the life of unglorified humanity upon this planet, will no longer be needed. This means there will be no clouds, or rain, or snow. Seasons, time distinctions, geographical boundaries, and the limitations of time and space in general will disappear in the grand eternal state. Glorified humanity will inhabit a glorified earth recreated and adapted to eternal conditions.

An immensely increased land surface will exist in the new and eternal earth as a result of the disappearance of the oceans. This will enable countless multitudes of glorified Israelites and Gentiles to people the new planet, which certainly will be a marvel of splendor.

But amazingly enough, the "new heaven" and "new earth" are not described, except in the matter of the absence of the sea. Concerning their appearance, size, and configuration, we shall have to wait until the day when we behold them in glory. Can they, however, be anything but glorious with God, the all-glorious Creator, in fullest manifestation, and with no sin, death, or evil of any kind to mar their perfection?

The New Jerusalem

Although the "new heaven" and the "new earth," as noted, are largely undescribed, the "new Jerusalem," which in eternity will be located on the new earth and form a vital part of it, is fully described. In the detailed description of the city's splendor is seen something of the glory of the new earth.

Both the new city and the new earth are presented in closest association with each other. The words of the seer emphasize this: "And I saw a new heaven and a new earth . . . And I John saw the holy city, new Jerusalem, coming down from God out of heaven" (Rev 21:1-2). New Jerusalem, pictured as descending out of heaven, most certainly takes up its abode on the new earth. This fact is suggested by the description given that it has foundations and gates through which people go in and out. This detail "is difficult to visualize unless the gates themselves rest on the earth."[3]

The city itself is a magnificent representation to finite minds of the infinite glory of the eternal home and destiny of the redeemed of all ages. New Jerusalem will be just as literal as the new earth, but both transcend our comprehension as unglorified saints, who have never experienced the eternal realm, where time and space and natural laws, as we now know them, will no longer exist.

The New Jerusalem symbolizes not only the home of the redeemed but the redeemed themselves occupying their home. In other words, the figure represents both the city and its inhabitants. Similarly, we think of New York, Paris, or Rome not only as a place of buildings, boulevards, and homes, but as a place inhabited by people.

Down through the centuries, God's saints have looked for such a city. By faith Abraham "was looking for the city which has foundations, whose architect and builder is God" (Heb 11:10, NASB). Concerning God's redeemed people, it is declared, "He has prepared a city for them" (Heb 11:16, NASB). "For here we do not have a lasting city, but we are seeking the city which is to come" (Heb 13:14, NASB).

Our Lord comforted His disciples upon His impending death and separation from them with the promise of the heavenly city. He declared, " 'In My Father's house are many dwelling places; if it were not so, I would have told you; for I go to prepare a place for you. And if I go and prepare a place for you, I will come again,

and receive you to Myself; that where I am, there you may be also' "
(Jn 14:2-3, NASB).

The City's Inhabitants

One of the principal inhabitants of the city is the glorified
church, the body and bride of Christ. When the angel would show
John "the bride, the wife of the Lamb," he showed him not a
woman, but "the holy city, Jerusalem, coming down out of heaven
from God" (Rev 21:9-10, NASB), "prepared as a bride adorned for
her husband" (Rev 21:2).

Christ went away to prepare the city principally for His bride,
the church, whom He "loved" and "gave Himself up for her; that
He might sanctify her, having cleansed her by the washing of water
with the word, that He might present to Himself the church in all
her glory, having no spot or wrinkle or any such thing; but that
she should be holy and blameless" (Eph 5:25-27, NASB).

So prominent will be the beloved bride and wife of the Lamb
in the New Jerusalem, that the city is identified with her, and called
"the bride," since her beauty and radiance never diminish, and
"the wife of the Lamb," because she is forever associated in glory
with her beloved Lord and Saviour.

But, as prominent as she is, the bride and body of Christ, "the
church of the firstborn" (Heb 12:23), is not the only inhabitant of
the holy city. God the Father will be present in full revelation of
divine light and glory (Rev 21:21), together with glorified Old
Testament, tribulation, and millennial saints, myriads of unfallen
angels, and our blessed Lord Himself (Heb 12:22-23).

God Tabernacles With Men

When the New Jerusalem takes up residence upon the earth, as
the eternal state dawns, God in unveiled glory will dwell among
men. John "heard a loud voice from the throne, saying, 'Behold, the
tabernacle of God is among men, and He shall dwell among them,
and they shall be His peoples, and God Himself shall be among
them' " (Rev 21:3, NASB).

God in His infinite holiness can now dwell among men, because Adam's curse has been removed, Satan and evil angels judged, the wicked punished, and the universe made sinless, except for "the lake of fire" (Rev 20:15; 21:8; 22:15).

In the kingdom, God tabernacled *over* His people (Rev 7:15, NASB). Now He can tabernacle *among* them, because the city is distinctively the "holy city" (Rev 21:10). The new heaven and the new earth are also holy, and all who occupy the New Jerusalem and the sin-cleansed universe are holy. Therefore, the city will have "the glory of God" and her brilliance will be as sparkling gems and the purest gold (Rev 21:9-14). This splendor will doubtlessly characterize also the new heaven and the new earth, with which the new city will be so inseparably connected.

The "tabernacle" of God with men "intimates that the saints will not settle permanently in the new earth, but move to and fro, visiting other parts of God's creation — His inheritance and ours" (Eph 1:10-11).[4]

God walked and talked with our unfallen parents in Eden. He appeared to the patriarchs of old in theophanies. He manifested His glory in the Shekinah glow in the holiest place in the inner sanctum of the tabernacle. He was revealed in Christ's sinless humanity in the days of His flesh. He indwells the church by His Spirit. But the actual dwelling of God with His redeemed and glorified creatures on earth awaits the fixed and holy eternal state.

Then He "who alone possesses immortality and dwells in unapproachable light" (1 Ti 6:16, NASB), shall reside intimately among His own, and "they shall be His peoples, and God Himself shall be among them" (Rev 21:3, NASB). The Shekinah glory of His presence shall fill and infuse the new city, the new heaven, and the new earth. The entire sin-cleansed universe shall be as the most holy place in the tabernacle of old. The glory and blessedness of this grand estate transcends the fondest hopes and dreams of the redeemed.

EARTH'S SORROWS GONE

In the eternal state, God "shall wipe away every tear." He does this because He will remove every cause and occasion of sorrow.

"There shall no longer be any death . . . any mourning, or crying, or pain: the first things have passed away" (Rev 21:4, NASB).

"The first things" are the sorrows and woes that belong to the first heaven and the first earth, ruined by sin. These things have no place in the new heaven and the new earth redeemed from sin and restored to fellowship with God.

Foremost among the sorrows sin has brought to the fallen race is death in a terrible threefold form. Spiritual death separates fallen man from fellowship with God. Physical death makes his earthly life short. Eternal death in Gehenna separates him forever from God.

But the grand note sounded in the new eternal order is "There shall no longer be any death." Spiritual death shall never again cause man to lose fellowship with God, because sin and all sinners will be confined to the lake of fire. Physical death will vanish, because the glorified bodies of the redeemed will be immortal. Eternal death, the lake of fire, will be cancelled by eternal life.

With death abolished, there will be no sickness, weakness, or infirmity. Mourning, crying, and pain will be banished. Belonging to the old fallen creation, they will pass away with it.

What a glorious prospect for all who put their trust in Christ. What a future of happiness and hope await all who flee to the Redeemer and accept the atonement He made possible by dying in our place. What joy to know one's sins are forgiven and that we are made fit to enter heaven and to have part in the holy city and the new earth.

WHAT IS HEAVEN?

As popularly used, the term *heaven* denotes the place and condition of the righteous in eternity in distinction to *hell,* the estate of the unrighteous. But Scripture speaks of the "third heaven," the ineffably glorious dwelling place of God (2 Co 12:2), called also "the heaven of heavens," that is, the highest heaven (1 Ki 8:27; 2 Ch 2:6). Hence, the first heaven, in Scripture, appears to be that of the clouds and the earth's atmosphere (Job 35:5), while the second heaven is that of the stars and planets (Gen 1:17; Deu 17:3).[5]

These two heavens are evidently made new for the eternal state (Rev 21:1). They must not be confused with the heaven of heavens, the third heaven, the dwelling place of God. "This latter subsists in moral and physical perfection, and undergoes no change."[6]

The righteous who die now go to God's presence in the third heaven (2 Co 5:2, 8; Phil 1:23). But the concept of heaven after the resurrection of the righteous and the dawn of eternity attains a much wider meaning than merely the third heaven. It will embrace the new heaven, the new earth, the New Jerusalem, and indeed a sinless universe.

In fact, in the eternal state, the term *heaven* will comprehend the entire universe, exclusive of the one isolation ward for all sinners, called Gehenna, or the lake of fire. This is why the Scriptures, in depicting the splendors of the world to come for the righteous on the closing pages of divine revelation, puncture the climactic and glorious account *three times* with a somber description and warning concerning eternal hell (Rev 21:8, 27; 22:15).

Heaven, as it has reference to the eternal state, may be defined as "a society of perfectly restored, unrestrained fellowship between God and man."[7] This fellowship, severed by sin, will in eternity be reestablished fully and completely.

Where, then, will heaven be? The answer: wherever God's presence and glory will be revealed. And this will be a glorious reality throughout the sinless universe. Not merely will the New Jerusalem descend "out of heaven," it will *be* heaven — "having the glory of God" and "her brilliance" like the sparkle of rarest gems and purest gold (Rev 21:10-21).

But not only will the New Jerusalem be heaven, in a most glorious sense, the new heaven and the new earth of the eternal state will be heaven too. They too will be sinless, and hence bathed and suffused in the light and splendor of God, unobscured by evil of any kind or tarnished by evildoers of any description.

And what is true of the New Jerusalem and the new heaven and new earth will be true of the entire universe. Sin and all sinners will be removed from it and eternally confined to one place in rigid separation from it. Therefore, the unveiled, infinite splendor of God can flood it and permeate every part of it as one grand temple of the living God.

When the Universe Becomes Paradise

The apostle Paul, on one occasion, was "caught up to the third heaven . . . into Paradise" (2 Co 12:2, 4, NASB). In the highest heavens, called by the Hebrews, "the heaven of heavens" (1 Ki 8:27; 2 Ch 2:6), God presently dwells and manifests His unveiled glory. Outside paradise, sin has been permitted and allowed to try angels and men. God's purpose is to deal with sin and sinners in such a way that He may be glorified in the eyes of all His creatures in the case of the righteous as well as the unrighteous.

Both the unfallen angels and redeemed men, who will occupy heaven, and the fallen angels and unredeemed men, who will be confined in hell, will vindicate God's love and holiness, His grace and His severity, His justness and righteousness.

In the sinless future God has in store for the holy angels and redeemed men, the limitless universe is to become one grand paradise. The boundless spheres of space are to be cleansed and constituted God's dwelling. There He will show forth His glory as He does now in the heaven of heavens.

No wonder no visible temple will be needed for the city of God, the New Jerusalem, nor for the new earth. God "all in all" will dwell in the midst of His holy angels and redeemed men. The blissful universe, cleansed of every defilement, will be one vast temple revealing and radiating God's unveiled presence (Rev 21:22). Ecstatic worship and unbroken communion of the creature with the Creator will make heaven universal. This will be possible because all sin and sinners will be confined in one place, never again to threaten the peace and destroy the serenity of God's illimitable spheres where righteousness will dwell (2 Pe 3:13).

Light Nevermore Invaded by Darkness

The city will have "no need of the sun or the moon to shine upon it," for it will be illuminated by "the glory of God" and "its lamp is the Lamb" (Rev 21:23). "And there shall no longer be any night; and they shall not have need of the light of a lamp nor the light of the sun, because the Lord God shall illumine them" (Rev 22:5, NASB). This also intimates that God's sinless order will radiate the glory of Him who declared: "I am the light of the world; he who follows Me shall not walk in the darkness, but shall have the light of life" (Jn 8:12, NASB).

In the sinless eternal state, the Lamb will give proof of this. Sun and moon as light giver and reflector will be superseded by the true light. As a result, the New Jerusalem's brilliance will be "like a very costly stone, as a stone of crystal-clear jasper" (Rev 21:11, NASB). The city being "pure gold, like clear glass" will be dazzling (Rev 21:18, NASB). Its twelve foundations garnished with multi-colored precious gems will be indescribably glorious (Rev. 21:19-21).

The nations, which will inhabit the new earth, shall walk in the light of the city and "the kings of the earth shall bring their glory into it" (Rev 21:24, NASB). The new earth itself will share a similar glory. No night shall be there. God's universe will be illuminated as the holy city will be.

Only one place in all the spheres of light will know darkness: that will be God's isolation ward for sin and all sinners. That doleful region of darkness will be a guarantee that the light that fills the rest of God's universe will never again be darkened by sin.

THE CLIMAX OF REDEMPTION'S WONDERS

The book of the Revelation (and with it divine revelation in general) ends in a burst of glory. The last chapter of the Bible is "descriptive of the consummation of the triumph and bliss of Christ's people with Him in the eternal kingdom of God."[8] The glorious destiny of the redeemed in their eternal blissful estate, is now blazoned forth in a climactic résumé (Rev 22:1-5).

Foremost is the "river of the water of life, clear as crystal, coming from the throne of God and of the Lamb" (Rev 22:1, NASB). This glorious stream symbolizes the outflow of perpetual spiritual blessing to all the redeemed now basking in the full glow of eternal life. The source is "the throne of God and of the Lamb," demonstrating that Christ still occupies the throne in the eternal state, "though the throne has a different character than during His mediatorial rule over the earth."[9]

Another marvel of the eternal state is the "tree of life," recalling the paradise of Eden before man's fall (Gen 3:22, 24). The plain indication is that the primeval condition of mankind before the fall is restored, but in a far greater and grander sense. The fruit of the tree of life symbolizes the fact that the curse of sin, involving death, has forever been banished.

The leaves of the tree of life are also said to be "for the healing of the nations." This cannot mean that pain and sickness exist, for these have been banished with the curse. This great fact of the removal of the curse of sin is, therefore, declared immediately following the statement about "healing," which here rather has the connotation of health-giving. "And there shall no longer be any curse" (Rev 22:3, NASB).

The leaves of the tree of life serve rather as a symbolic reminder of "the sickness from which the nations *had* suffered during their *earthly* life, but shall never suffer again in the new earth."[10]

Another marvel of the eternal state is that God's redeemed will enjoy blissful activity. There will be no inane sitting on the edge of a cloud and dangling one's feet in purposeless inactivity. The thrill of the eternal order is that there will be meaningful ministration, not *work,* which is the result of the curse.

The stirring declaration that looms with infinite possibilities of joy is that God's "servants shall serve Him." At one stroke is removed the threat of any boredom in eternity. After all, eternity is a long time for even the most ecstatic pleasures to grow dim. But being assured the status of servants of God and having the assurance of endless variety of ministry for Him, at once makes the prospect of heaven entrancingly attractive.

THE CAPSTONE OF ETERNAL BLESSEDNESS

The account of "all that God has prepared for those who love Him" (1 Co 2:9, NASB) rises to a great crescendo as it comes to its grand finale. John the apostle, by the Spirit of prophecy, adds the few concluding touches to the magnificent scene of endless bliss that is to be the eternal portion of the redeemed.

"And they shall see His face, and His name shall be on their foreheads" (Rev 22:4, NASB). Could anything be more sublime and more utterly satisfying for the redeemed than to enjoy the sheer delight of unbroken fellowship with God in immediate and completely unobstructed access to the divine glory? "They shall see His face," that is, see Him in all His splendor and glory, gaze upon His countenance, and behold His beauty forever. No greater joy or exhilarating thrill will be vouchsafed the creature than to look in rapt worship and adoration upon the face of the Creator-Redeemer.

The apostle had this wondrous experience in mind when he wrote concerning one day seeing the Lord face to face and being like Him. "See how great a love the Father has bestowed upon us, that we should be called children of God; and such we are. . . . Beloved, now are we the children of God, and it has not appeared as yet what we shall be. We know that, if He should appear, we shall be like Him, because we shall see Him just as He is" (1 Jn 3:1-2, NASB).

But seeing Him and being like Him constitute only part of the unending joys that await the saints in the eternal state. His name is declared to be "on their foreheads." This beautiful imagery indicates that the glorified saints belong to Him in a most wonderful and blessed way (cf. Rev 2:17; 3:12; 7:3; 14:1).

Then John repeats a fact that he has already stressed concerning eternity (cf. Rev 21:22-24). He does so, no doubt, because the wondrous illumination and sheer brilliance of a sinless environment were overpowering in the vision of the future granted him. "And there shall no longer be any night; and they shall not have need of the light of a lamp nor the light of the sun, because the Lord God shall illumine them" (Rev 22:5, NASB).

THE CROWNING WONDER OF ALL

The apostle John, by inspiration, gives the last touch, the most wonderful of all, to the magnificent prophetic portrait of the eternal state of the righteous. Not only will the redeemed serve God, see

His face, have His name on their foreheads, and be illuminated by the ineffable light of His immediate presence. "They shall reign forever and ever" (Rev 22:5, NASB). They shall be associated with Him in the administration of the new order His wisdom and grace have brought into being in a sin-cleansed universe.

It is wonderful enough that we are told "His servants shall serve Him," but to be told that these same servants shall also reign with Him, is beyond our finite minds to comprehend. Servants of our glorious God, in the eternal glories He has prepared for His own, will actually be kings.

Even now in a world marred by sin and sinners, the lowliest servant of God is in reality a king. What will it be in the eternal world, where righteousness shall dwell and sinners will forever be removed? Then God's servants will have the dignity and honor of their Creator-Redeemer imparted to them, so that their every service will be performed to God's glory in regal splendor.

"We shall be like Him, because we shall see Him just as He is" (1 Jn 3:2, NASB). We shall "reign forever and ever"! *Hallelujah!*

15

Don't Fall into the Occult Trap

THE SURVEY OF BIBLICAL PROPHECY set forth in the preceding pages ends on such a climactic note of joyful triumph that I was tempted to stop there. With a sinless universe filled with holy angels and happy redeemed and glorified men, bathed in God's glory and ecstatically worshiping and serving their Creator, it seemed anticlimactic to attempt to add anything to so blissful a scene. Indeed, nothing can be added to it.

God's revelation ends in a burst of glory and finality. All His wondrous plans and purposes for the earth, man, and the universe, as predicted throughout the Word, are seen to be fully accomplished in the last pages of Holy Scripture.

SOUND AN ALARM

But what can and must be added to the portrait of prophecy presented in the Word is a warning of the growing peril of occult deception in the world today. The danger faced is intensified by the fact that approaching world cataclysm is stimulating new interest in knowing the future, both of people and nations. As a result, astrologers, witches, fortune-tellers, and prophets of every description abound on every hand. The situation steadily grows more ominous.

Denials of the full inspiration and authority of Scripture are becoming more pronounced and popular. As a consequence, men's interest and attention are being turned away from Holy Scripture and its forecast of the future. The result is that multitudes are being exposed to every false prophet and prognosticator of the future that comes their way and left a helpless prey to the occult charlatans of the day.

BEWARE OF IGNORANCE

The toll exacted by ignorance is appalling in any realm, particularly the religious. Ignorance regarding the Word of God and its warning concerning the danger of the sphere of evil supernaturalism is to a large degree responsible for the occult boom of our day. Through neglect and rejection of God's Word, people are being exposed to the delusions of spiritualism, astrology, magic, fortune-telling, and particularly demonized religionism, parading under the guise of Christianity.

The apostle Paul, by prophetic inspiration, foresaw this perilous state of affairs of the end time preceding the Lord's coming. In 2 Timothy, chapter 3, a most amazing revelation of conditions rapidly crystallizing in our day, the apostle alerts God's people against the peril of ignorance. His words are incisive. "This know also, that in the last days perilous times shall come" (2 Ti 3:1). The New American Standard Bible renders, "But realize this, that in the last days difficult times will come."

Unless we know the Word of God, we shall never realize the gravity of the occult delusion that is settling upon our world today and the peril it presents to mankind.

RECOGNIZE THE FRUIT OF OCCULT DELUSION

Abandonment of the Word of God and the substitution of demonized religionism for biblical Christianity is having its fearful effects upon society in general. The apostle describes our occult era in prophetic vision. It is as if he lived now and read our daily newspapers with their endless tale of crime, war, violence, and immorality.

"For men will be lovers of self, lovers of money, boastful, arrogant, revilers, disobedient to parents, ungrateful, unholy, unloving, irreconcilable, malicious gossips, without self-control, brutal, haters of good, treacherous, reckless, conceited, lovers of pleasure rather than lovers of God; holding to a form of godliness although they have denied its power" (2 Ti 3:2-5, NASB).[1]

The most revealing declaration of the apostle Paul is that in the occult age we have now entered, men are holding to a mere empty form of religion, having renounced its spiritual dynamic because of denial of the Person and redemptive work of Christ. This tragic state, so widespread in the apostasy of the end time, constitutes an open door to demonic incursion and the cultivation of spiritism and spiritistic cults in the place of sound biblical Christianity.

The moral instability of such apostate leaders is underscored by the apostle. "For among them are those who enter into households and captivate weak women weighed down with sins, led on by various impulses" (v. 6, NASB). Likewise their intellectual and spiritual blindness is exposed. They are declared to be "always learning," getting one academic degree after another, yet "never able to come to the knowledge of the truth" of God's Word (v.7).

Avoid Occult Contamination

The apostle enjoins strict separation from apostates and occultists as well as those who are deluded by them and led into demonized religionism and resulting lawless conduct. The injunction is forceful in its terseness: "From such turn away" (2 Ti 3:5).

The importance of this command can scarcely be exaggerated. God's people must separate themselves from wickedness of every sort, particularly from the evil of occultism. Implication by direct contact with the occult arts, such as spiritism, magic, astrology, and fortune-telling, exposes one to demon power and bondage.

Implication in occultism, however, may also result by indirect contact through religion, either in spiritistically oriented pagan religions or in the perversions of Christianity. In the case of the latter, unbiblical doctrines and consequent erroneous practices open the door to demon intrusion, marring and obscuring the work of the Holy Spirit, or snaring the victim in error and cultism, or in some form of fanaticism.

The apostle illustrates the peril of occult religion by an allusion to the magicians of Egypt, Jannes and Jambres. These names do not actually occur in the Old Testament, but are preserved in Hebrew extrabiblical tradition as opposers of Moses when he stood before Pharaoh. "Just as Jannes and Jambres opposed Moses," so, the apostle declares, occult religionists of the last days will "oppose the truth." They are characterized as "men of depraved mind, rejected as regards the faith" (2 Ti 3:8, NASB).

To a certain degree, Jannes and Jambres of the court of Egypt were able by demon power to imitate Moses, the man of God, who performed miracles by the power of God. These powerful sorcerers and magicians could turn a staff into a serpent, change the waters of the Nile to blood, and bring forth frogs (Ex 7:11-12, 21-22; 8:7). However, they could not convert dust into gnats, as God's servant did, and so had to acknowledge "the finger of God" and abjectly confess their own limitation (Ex 8:18-19).

Jannes and Jambres furnish an example of the type of occult workers of the last days who will operate in the realm of evil supernaturalism under the guise of religion. In the case of apostates and cultists, they operate under the mask of Christianity, but deny the essential and foundational truths of the faith.

But these occult workers will ultimately be exposed for what they really are, as were the magicians of Egypt. "But they will not make further progress; for their folly will be obvious to all, as also that of those two came to be" (2 Ti 3:9, NASB).

Follow Sound Doctrine

The Word of God, the Holy Scripture, correctly interpreted and faithfully followed, is the only sure protection against demon incursion and delusion.[2] This fact needs special emphasis in the perilous times in which we live. Today in many Christian circles, there is a growing tendency to place experience before doctrine. Certain experiences are sought and promoted with apparently little concern to the question, What do the Scriptures *really* teach on the matter?

At the same time as apostasy increases, conviction on doctrinal issues is waning in many evangelical circles. This is a dangerous trend in an age when demon activity is accelerating. Unless sound doctrine is adhered to, demonic powers can enter and imitate the gifts of the Holy Spirit.

The apostle Paul foresaw this danger at the end time. Significantly and purposely, he places doctrine *before* experience in this pivotal chapter which deals with the ministry of the Word of God in the age of the occult.

To Timothy he declared: "But you followed my teaching [doctrine], conduct, purpose, faith, patience, love, perseverance, persecutions, sufferings" (2 Ti 3:10-11, NASB).

BE OBEDIENT TO THE WORD

Two requirements must be followed if the believer is to escape the snare of the demonic in the age of the occult. First, he must desire to know exactly what the Word of God reveals on the matter. Second, he must be willing to believe and follow exactly what the Word reveals.

Such fidelity to the Word in the apostle's case was proved by his willingness to endure persecutions and sufferings for his adherence to the Word and will of God. He mentions the "persecutions" and "sufferings" that came to him "at Antioch, at Iconium and at Lystra; what persecutions I endured and out of them all the Lord delivered me!" (2 Ti 3:11, NASB).

The apostle's fidelity to the Word was also attested by his godly, well-regulated life. He was free of confusion and spiritual lawlessness that characterize believers who fall prey to false doctrine and land in some cult or error. "And indeed, all who desire to live godly in Christ Jesus will be persecuted" (2 Ti 3:12).

Meanwhile, those who have no keen desire to know what the Word teaches and hence have no solid foundation to obey the truth, will go on "deceiving and being deceived" (v. 13).

Tragically, this process of deception not only occurs in "evil men and impostors" who are apostates and consciously reject God's truth, it may take place also in truly born-again believers, who through unconscious ignorance of God's Word, are exploited by Satan and demons. Satanic strategy is to inflict harm on anyone, believers included, who do not arm themselves with the full panoply of the Word.

Continue in Sound Christian Faith

Paul's warning to Timothy is especially relevant in an age of the rise of sects and movements that advertise some new revelation, or some new truth, or experience, supposedly lost during the Christian centuries and allegedly recovered recently by certain groups.

Strangely enough, the apostle did not tell Timothy to seek some new path. Rather, he urged him to cling to the old and tried ways.

"You, however, continue in the things you have learned and become convinced of, knowing from whom you have learned them; and that from childhood you have known the sacred writings which are able to give you the wisdom that leads to salvation through faith which is in Christ Jesus" (2 Ti 3:14-15, NASB).

Dare to Give the Word First Place

The danger of demonic delusion at the end of the age called forth the central passage of the Bible on the inspiration and authority of Holy Scripture. "All Scripture is inspired by God" (2 Ti 3:16, NASB). Since the entire Bible is literally "God-breathed" (*theopneustos,* Greek) it is completely authoritative and to be considered final in all questions of Christian doctrine and conduct.

Accordingly, Holy Scripture is to be given the place of absolute precedence in the believer's life and experience. It is to be viewed as "profitable" in the sense of beneficial. It preserves the believer from worldliness, sin, and satanic delusion. It also trains him in righteousness, "that the man of God may be adequate, equipped for every good work" (v. 17, NASB).

It is significant that once again (as in v. 10) the apostle gives "teaching" (doctrine) the precedence. Unwavering loyalty to God's Word and deep conviction of the truth and authority of its teaching results in Christian doctrine. This forms the foundation for any firm building of Christian experience and character. It constitutes the only sure bulwark against error and demonic intrusion and despoilment.

Such Bible doctrine is valuable for "reproof" and "correction." Both of these benefits are so necessary in a day when "the Spirit explicitly says . . . some will fall away from the faith, paying attention to deceitful spirits and doctrines of demons" (1 Ti 4:1, NASB), and when God's "beloved" are pressured to "believe every spirit" rather than to "test the spirits whether they are from God" (1 Jn 4:1, NASB).

Only as the believer heeds God's voice through the Scripture and meticulously follows its doctrinal teaching will he be able to receive reproof where his experience fails to measure up to God's Word and so correct his conduct. Only in this way can he be trained "in righteousness." Only as his experience and conduct conform to the Word of God will he be freed and made immune to demonic deception and despoilment.

In concluding this warning and plea to God's people, I can do no better than to declare what I enunciated more than two decades ago in the first printing of *Biblical Demonology*. "In the midst of this appalling confusion of modern cults and the innumerable sects of Christianity, the Bible, God's living Word of Truth, is the Christian's only sure protection against doctrinal deception, and demonic despoliation — the Bible rightly understood, however, and implicitly obeyed. Satan and his hosts can bypass human opinions and men's interpretations, but *they cannot penetrate the impregnable defense of God's Holy Word!*"[3]

In an age of increasing deception, may our motto be: "To the law and to the testimony: if they speak not according to this word, it is because there is no light in them" (Is 8:20).

NOTES

CHAPTER 1

1. For a good summary of the present-day occult explosion introducing the occult age, see "The Age of the Occult," *McCall's*, March 1970, pp. 61-65. See also "The Quest for Spiritual Survival," *Life*, Jan. 9, 1970, pp. 16-20, 30.
2. James A. Pike and Diane Kennedy Pike, *The Other Side* (New York: Doubleday, 1968); Allen Spraggett, *The Bishop Pike Story* (New York: New Amer. Lib., 1970); Merrill F. Unger, *The Haunting of Bishop Pike* (Wheaton, Ill.: Tyndale, 1971).
3. *McCall's*, March 1970, p. 76.
4. *Life*, Jan. 9, 1970, p. 23.
5. Raphael Gasson, *The Challenging Counterfeit* (Plainfield, N.J.: Logos, 1966).

CHAPTER 2

1. Wilbur M. Smith, *World Crises and the Prophetic Scriptures* (Chicago: Moody, 1950), pp. 319-50.
2. Merrill F. Unger, *Biblical Demonology* (Wheaton, Ill.: Scripture Press, 1952).
3. Unger, *Demons in the World Today* (Wheaton, Ill.: Tyndale, 1971), pp. 1-209.
4. For a description of white versus black magic, see ibid., pp. 75-99.
5. See Unger, *The Haunting of Bishop Pike*, pp. 1-115. For the bishop's own account of his abandonment of revealed Christianity and his lapse into the occult, see James A. Pike and Diane Kennedy Pike, *The Other Side*, pp. 1-325.
6. For accounts of demon possession and inhabitation in nineteenth-century China, see John L. Nevius, *Demon Possession and Allied Themes*, 5th ed. (Westwood, N.J.: Revell). See also *Demon Experiences in Many Lands* (Chicago: Moody, 1960).
7. See "The Age of the Occult," *McCall's*, March 1970, pp. 61-65.
8. Ibid., pp. 74-75, 133-36.
9. Cf. Brad Steiger, *Sex and Satanism* (New York, Ace: 1969).

CHAPTER 3

1. *Encyclopaedia Britannica*, 1964, ed., s.v. "Ecumenical Movement."
2. S. C. Neil, *Towards Church Union 1937-1952* (1952); *The Ten Formative Years*, (World Council, 1948); *The Church, the Churches, and the World Council of Churches* (World Council, 1950); N. Goodall, *The Ecumenical Movement* (Toronto: Oxford, 1961).
3. *Reader's Digest*, October 1971, p. 95.
4. Ibid.
5. Ibid., p. 100.
6. John F. Walvoord, "Where Is the Modern Church Going?" in *Prophecy and the Seventies*, ed. Charles Lee Feinberg (Chicago: Moody, 1971), pp. 116-17.

CHAPTER 4

1. William F. Arndt and F. Wilbur Gingrich, *A Greek-English Lexicon of the New Testament*, (Chicago: U. Chicago, 1957), p. 108.
2. *Theological Dictionary of the New Testament*, ed. Gerhard Kittel (Grand Rapids: Eerdmans, 1968), p. 743.
3. Arndt and Gingrich, p. 743.
4. Charles C. Ryrie, *The Bible and Tomorrow's News* (Wheaton, Ill.: Scripture Press, 1971), p. 127.
5. Cf. Dwight Pentecost, *Will Man Survive?* (Chicago: Moody, 1971), pp. 155-56.
6. John F. Walvoord, "Why Must Christ Return?" in *Prophecy and the Seventies*, p. 38.
7. Hal Lindsey with C. C. Carlson, *The Late Great Planet Earth* (Grand Rapids: Zondervan, 1971), p. 143.
8. Ibid., p. 143.
9. Ibid., p. 145.

CHAPTER 5

1. Stephen F. Olford, "The Judgment Seat of Christ," in *Prophecy and the Seventies*, p. 66.
2. Henry Varley, *Christ's Coming Kingdom* (London: Whiting, 1886), p. 256.
3. Unger, *Great Neglected Bible Prophecies* (Wheaton, Ill.: Scripture Press, 1955), p. 115.
4. Joseph Henry Thayer, *Greek-English Lexicon of the New Testament* (New York: Harper, 1889), p. 652.
5. Richard Chenevix Trench, *Synonyms of the New Testament* (Grand Rapids: Eerdmans, 1947), p. 79.

CHAPTER 6

1. Charles C. Ryrie, *The Bible and Tomorrow's News*, p. 35.
2. John F. Walvoord, *Daniel — Key to Prophetic Revelation* (Chicago: Moody, 1971), pp. 228-37.
3. Clarence Larkin, *Dispensational Truth*, 7th ed. (Philadelphia: Larkin Estate, 1920), p. 67.
4. Walvoord, *The Nations in Prophecy* (Grand Rapids: Zondervan, 1971), p. 92.
5. These words are an adaptation from Jean Monnet, called "the father of the Common Market," in "Mister Europe at Eighty" in *Look*, November 1968.
6. *Encyclopaedia Britannica*, 1964 ed., s.v. "Economic Union."
7. See "Europe's Dreams of Unity Revive," *Time*, July 4, 1969.

CHAPTER 7

1. *Gesenius' Hebrew-English Lexicon*, ed. Edward Robinson (London: Samuel Bagster, 1882), p. 955.
2. *Encyclopaedia Britannica*, 1965 ed., s.v. "Russia."
3. S. R. Driver, *The Book of Genesis* (London, 1904), p. 115; Unger, *Archaeology and the Old Testament* (Grand Rapids: Zondervan, 1954), p. 80.
4. *Encyclopedia Americana*, 1951 ed., s.v. "Gyges."
5. Herodotus. 1:103-106.
6. W. F. Albright, "Recent Discoveries in Bible Lands," in *Young's Analytical Concordance to the Bible*, 20th ed. (New York, 1936), p. 32.
7. Nelson Glueck, *The Other Side of the Jordan* (New Haven, Conn.: Amer. Schools of Oriental Res., 1940), p. 93.
8. For a correct interpretation of Daniel 11:40-45, see William Kelly, *Notes on the Book of Daniel*, 7th ed. (New York: Loizeaux, 1949), pp. 234-39.

CHAPTER 8

1. Ross Terrill, *800,000,000 — The Real China* (Boston: Atlantic Monthly, 1972), p. 235.
2. "Problems of War and Strategy" in *Quotations from Chairman Mao Tse-Tung, Selected Works,* 11 (Nov. 6, 1938): 224.
3. *Time,* May 21, 1965, p. 35.
4. Hal Lindsey and C. C. Carlson, *The Late Great Planet Earth,* p. 87.
5. J. Dwight Pentecost, *Will Man Survive?,* p. 127.
6. Terrill, p. 218.
7. Cf. Pentecost, p. 131.

CHAPTER 9

1. See Mal Couch, "The Amazing Rise of Israel" in *Dimension for Better Living,* (Chicago: Moody Monthly, 1972).
2. Cleveland Amory, "Israel in Siege," *Reader's Digest,* April 1970, pp. 147-54.
3. J. Dwight Pentecost, *Will Man Survive?* p. 89.

CHAPTER 10

1. "Nixon Talks About War," *U.S. News and World Report,* May 15, 1972, p. 100.
2. Ibid.
3. "Slowing Down the Arms Race," *Time,* June 5, 1972, p. 18.
4. *Encyclopaedia Britannica,* 1964 ed., s.v. "Zionism."

CHAPTER 11

1. For a comprehensive study of the kingdom, see John F. Walvoord, *The Millennial Kingdom* (Findlay, Ohio: Dunham, 1959); and George N. H. Peters, *The Theocratic Kingdom,* 3 vols. (Grand Rapids: Kregel, 1952).
2. Walvoord, *The Nations in Prophecy* (Grand Rapids: Zondervan, 1971), p. 157.
3. Ibid.
4. Cf. J. Dwight Pentecost, *Will Man Survive?* pp. 172-74.
5. Walvoord, *The Millennial Kingdom,* p. 228.

CHAPTER 12

1. *Encyclopedia Americana,* 1951 ed., s.v. "Utopia."
2. Lyndon B. Johnson, "America at the Crossroads," *Reader's Digest,* March 1969, p. 56.
3. Ibid., p. 55.
4. Carl T. Rowan and David Mazie, "Hunger — It's Here Too," *Reader's Digest,* November 1968, p. 128.
5. J. Dwight Pentecost, *Will Man Survive?* p. 186.

CHAPTER 13

1. For more on the subject of the confirmed depravity of fallen angels, see Merrill F. Unger, *Biblical Demonology,* pp. 215-16.
2. See Unger, *Zechariah: Prophet of Messiah's Glory,* 2d. ed. (Grand Rapids: Zondervan, 1970), pp. 224-25.
3. Norman B. Harrison, *The End — Re-Thinking the Revelation* (Minneapolis, Minn.: Harrison Serv., 1941), p. 181.
4. W. Kelly, *The Revelation Expounded,* 5th ed. (London: F. E. Race, 1921), p. 230.
5. H. A. Ironside, *Lectures on the Revelation* (New York: Loizeaux, 1930), p. 330.
6. See Unger, *Demons in the World Today,* p. 162.
7. F. C. Jennings, *Satan: His Person, Work, Place, and Destiny* (New York: A. C. Gaebelein, n.d.), pp. 228-29.

CHAPTER 14

1. Walter Scott, *Exposition of the Revelation of Jesus Christ,* 4th ed. (London: Pickering & Inglis, n.d.), p. 418.
2. Norman B. Harrison, *The End — Rethinking the Revelation,* p. 202.
3. John F. Walvoord, *The Revelation of Jesus Christ* (Chicago: Moody, 1969), p. 324.
4. Scott, p. 422.
5. See *New Scofield Reference Bible* (New York: Oxford, 1967), p. 1261.
6. Scott, p. 417.
7. Harrison, p. 203.
8. Henry Alford, *The Greek New Testament,* rev. Everett F. Harrison (Chicago: Moody, 1958), 4:736.
9. Walvoord, p. 329.
10. Friedrich Duesterdieck, quoted in Erich Sauer, *The Triumph of the Crucified* (London: Paternoster, 1951), p. 199.

CHAPTER 15

1. Cf. Tim LaHaye, *The Beginning of the End* (Wheaton, Ill.: Tyndale, 1972), pp. 113-23.
2. Cf. Merrill F. Unger, *Biblical Demonology,* pp. 179-80.
3. Ibid.